1783 { GLASGOW'S HERALD } 1983

Original perspective drawing by Charles Rennie Mackintosh
for the Glasgow Herald buildings in Mitchell Street, 1893.

1783 {GLASGOW'S HERALD} 1983

ALASTAIR PHILLIPS

RICHARD DREW PUBLISHING
GLASGOW

British Library Cataloguing in Publication Data

Phillips, Alastair
  Glasgow's Herald 1783–1983.
  1. Glasgow Herald – History
  I. Title
  072′.91443   PN5139.G/

  ISBN 0-86267-008-X

First published 1982 by
Richard Drew Publishing Ltd
20 Park Circus, Glasgow G3 6BE, Scotland

Editor: Antony Kamm
Designed by James W Murray

ISBN (limp edition) 0 86267 008 X
     (luxury edition) 0 86267 009 8
     (limited edition) 0 86267 010 1

Set in Century by John Swain & Son, Glasgow

Printed and bound in Great Britain by ©ollins, Glasgow

Contents

Acknowledgments

The author has drawn heavily on the work of legions of staff writers and researchers, few of whom can be acknowledged by name since for the first 175 years of the existence of the Glasgow Herald all contributions by staff were anonymous. Substantial reference has also been made to R.M.W. Cowan's D.Litt. thesis 'The Newspaper in Scotland 1815–1860'; to Alexander Sinclair's 'Fifty Years of Newspaper Life'; and to Dr John Strang's 'Glasgow and its Clubs'.

The Glasgow Herald would like to acknowledge the help and encouragement given by many people in the research for this book, in particular:

Marie Jordan and Herald librarians – Marie Campbell; Stroma Fraser; Catherine Turner; Kenneth Wright; John Dalziel; Annie Cunningham; Christopher Boyce; Margaret Ball.

Bill Doig and Herald picture librarians – Robert Tweedie; Jim McNeish; Malcolm Beaton; Anthony Murray.

Doug Bottomley and Herald photographers – John Mackay; Arthur Kinloch; Edward Jones; James Millar; Stuart Paterson; James Connor; Ian Hossack; James Thomson; Duncan Dingsdale.

Isabel Barnes; Alison Brady; Eve Jarvie; Arlene Thomson; Susan Ward.

Mr Joe Fisher and the Glasgow Room staff of the Mitchell Library; Mr Richard Dell and staff of the Strathclyde Archives department; Miss Pamela Reekie, of the Hunterian Museum, Glasgow University; Professor Anthony Jones and his staff, Glasgow School of Art; Paul Cowan, for his microfilm work; and photographer Harry Turner.

Foreword

by Arnold Kemp
Editor of the Glasgow Herald

If there is nothing as stale as yesterday's newspaper, then there are few curiosities as fascinating as a really old one. Most of us have experienced the pleasure of coming upon a yellowed paper while engaged on some useful task, such as lifting the carpet, and then finding that time has flown in the perusal of forgotten events. Newspapers on file are a unique record of the concerns, prejudices and misconceptions of the passing times. Their typographical dress changes, they move up and down the market (in the jargon of the trade), they support this political party or that, they adjust to the changing tastes of the generations, but their central purposes do not vary much, though since the early days they have become less important as purveyors of primary news: radio and television do that much faster.

Once upon a time newspapers enjoyed an undesirable amount of power, which they could sometimes use unscrupulously. One recalls the famous exchange of cables in 1897 between the American publisher William Randolph Hearst and the artist Frederick Remington who had been sent to Havana to help foment the Spanish-American War.

Remington: 'Everything is quiet. There is no trouble here. There will be no war. I wish to return.'

Hearst: 'Please remain. You furnish the pictures and I'll furnish the war.'

Lord Haldane was hounded out of public life during the First World War by The Times because of his interest in German culture. Now that the consumer of news has a multiple choice among TV, radio and the Press, the opportunities for distortion and manipulation have been reduced, if not removed altogether.

This is no matter for regret, but in any case the Glasgow Herald has ploughed an honourable furrow through its two centuries. The strength of its reputation is a tribute to the industry and integrity of my predecessors, so delightfully chronicled in this book. Perhaps because the Herald's readership depended very much on accurate commercial information, reliability was something without which success would not have been possible. That does not make it any the less to be valued. But it is not enough, in journalism, to be reliable. In the old days editors were also polemical and vitriolic to a degree that might shock the modern reader. Today there is rather less emphasis on dignity and more on entertainment.

A Herald reader in the shape of a nineteenth-century tobacco jar. Unfortunately the same figure can be seen reading other papers. The Victoria and Albert Museum has one reading The Times.

It would be pleasant, at all times, to be right about the big things. This is the really difficult part of editorship, and the Herald, like all other papers, will have been wrong as well as right about trends and events on which history will more surely pass judgment. It is a matter of great pride when retrospection shows us to have been right about Chamberlain and Munich, in the teeth of powerful opposition.

Reading about the great editors of the past fills one with not a little awe. They were often august and dignified; Alastair Phillips presents them not as remote personages but as human beings. According to the book, it was Alastair Warren who was the first Editor to be called by his Christian name by most of his staff, and that is in keeping with the contemporary spirit. And that leads one to the reflection, as one ponders the varied men who pass through the pages of the book, that an editor's style must reflect his personality; it must flow from his own nature. A sociable and gregarious editor who tries to be august and remote will make himself and his staff unhappy; a reserved personality will keep a distance.

The book demonstrates also that editors down the years have remarkably similar problems. These relate to that distasteful commodity, money, about which most editors would really rather forget, a tendency which makes our friends in the commercial departments prone to despair. Yet it is a problem for all, how to manage a part of the job for which they may have little taste by temperament and which is alien to those talents that took them to the editorial chair. It is the journalism that is the fun and the glory of our industry which is of a kind going out of fashion. It employs many people and has another unusual characteristic in that almost every person who works in the industry may become vital at some point in the productive cycle, from those who write the words, or move them around, or send them flying across the wires, or make the mighty presses thunder (still one of the most thrilling sights of all), to those who contrive the paper to turn up with the milk in the morning so routinely that the reader never bothers his head how it got there. It is a mosaic of people doing their different jobs. And if that makes us very vulnerable to industrial action, it also means that we are a community in which every member is dependent, at some point, on the others.

Editors may be popular and approachable, like Warren, impressive and formidable like Robieson, stalking the clubs and corridors of powers like Bruce, or convivial men-about-town like Samuel Hunter. But beneath them – in the early days consigned to obscurity but within more recent memory more clearly seen if still somewhat in the shadows – are the thousands of people who toil under them. It is customary to say that newspapers no longer possess among their staff as many characters as once they did. This seems to be said by each generation of the last, and is never true. Looking round the Glasgow Herald today, I do not detect a shortage of characters, though discretion forbids their inclusion in any contemporary history. But through the two hundred years, starting with the founder Mennons himself, much of the history of this newspaper has been a history about people. And that is the chief delight of Alastair Phillips' book: that it does not languish in the morass of footling information in which official histories sometimes become stuck. Rather it glories in the frailties and foibles of the people themselves, at first the principals but later, where memory reaches, about some of the folk who made the paper what it was and is.

Editors should be humble. There was a story told about the old Manchester Guardian when the night editor, after seeing the pages away from the composing room, would retire to his desk and, when satisfied with the page proofs, press a button which rang a bell in the machine-room authorising the machines to be started.

After doing this for about ten years, he was disconcerted one night to find the messenger delivering the papers before he had pressed the button. When he protested, he was told that it had been disconnected these five years past.

Finally, my sincere thanks to John Weyers, Associate Editor of the Glasgow Herald, for nursing the book through its many stages, posthumously to Anthony Finlay, Executive Editor of the Glasgow Herald until his tragic death this year, who took a keen interest in the project, and to our congenial collaborator Antony Kamm, editorial consultant to Richard Drew Publishing Ltd.

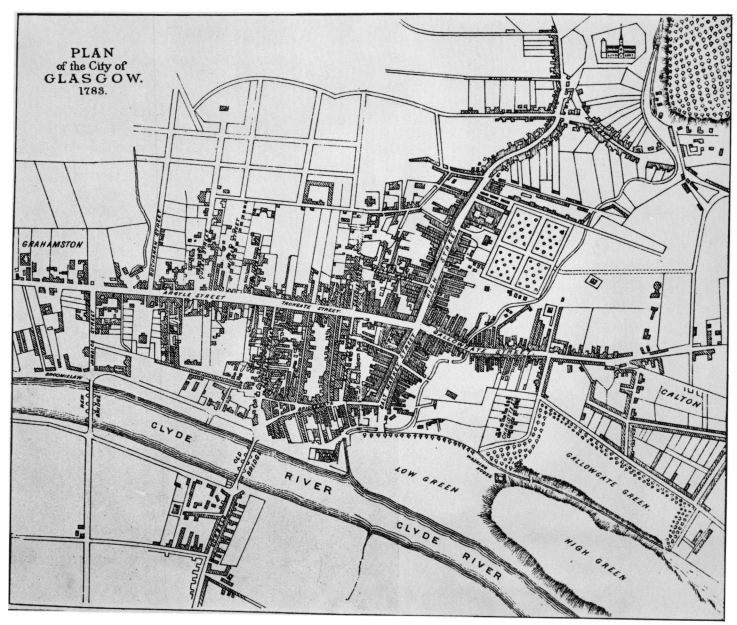

Glasgow in 1783 – the year of the
Herald's foundation as the Glasgow
Advertiser.

chapter 1

IN THE BEGINNING

GIVE OR TAKE just a few hours, the Glasgow Herald is the same age as the United States of America.

During the middle days of January 1783, while the Powers at Versailles were putting the finishing touches to the document that would give the revolted colonies their official independence, in Glasgow John Mennons, a printer but lately come to Glasgow from Edinburgh to seek, or rather to improve, his fortune, was laying out the first edition of the newspaper he intended to launch upon the commercial capital of the West. But he was not yet quite ready to lock up the last forme. He still lacked his lead story. It was, however, worth waiting for, and might reasonably be identified as the weightiest newspaper scoop of the succeeding two hundred years. It came on the eve of publication, when the Lord Provost sent round to him a copy of a personal letter he had just received – no doubt by fast horseman – from Lord Grantham, the Foreign Secretary. The message read:

John Mennons

My Lord,

I have the satisfaction to acquaint your Lordship that a messenger is just arrived from Paris with the preliminary Articles between Great Britain and France and between Great Britain and Spain were (sic) signed at Versailles by Mr Fitzherbert his Majesty's Minister Plenipotentiary and the Ministers Plenipotentiary of the aforesaid Courts. The preliminaries with Holland are not yet signed, but a Cessation of Hostilities is agreed upon.

I send your Lordship immediate notice of this important event, that it may be made public to the City without loss of time.

Grantham

Newspapers in those days were not as demonstrative as they have since become. John Mennons did not make this the lead on his front page but, using it is true the larger of the two type-faces in his printer's case, he placed it in the middle of the third of the four columns on the back page. Indeed, it might even seem that this 'most agreeable intelligence received by express', was doubly welcome since it filled a space which had been reserved for a late story that did not turn up; the sort of crisis well-known to editors and chief sub-editors to this day. The historic despatch was preceded by a note which read: 'We are sorry to have to inform the public that thro' an unforeseen accident, the private intelligence due by this day's post has not come.'

Observe how from the start the Herald has taken readers into its confidence.

And so the Glasgow Advertiser and the intimation of the new America burst simultaneously upon the bien merchants of the Saltmarket on the morning of 27 January 1783.

But this was the Glasgow of the Tobacco Barons and for them this was no joyous coincidence. To quote from 'Senex', a venerable contributor in the paper in a later generation:

Well do I remember the melancholy and dejected countenance of every person in our city at the sad news of the loss of America; and the circumstance is still fresh in my memory of my father, almost with tears in his eyes, reading to us all the first number of the Glasgow Advertiser published by Mennons in which at full length were recorded the preliminaries of peace between Great Britain and the United States.

There were no rejoicing here at this peace, no illuminations, no bonfires, no squibs or crackers, no firing of guns or ringing of bells – all was silence and sorrow; even child as I then was, I was like to cry because the Americans had beaten us.

Nor did it sweeten the dose that one of the more prominent Glasgow traders, Robert Oswald, a friend of both Franklin and Adams, was, at

The Trongate in 1783.

least in the preliminaries, the sole British Commissioner at Versailles.

In those circumstances this might hardly seem to be a propitious beginning – unless one adheres to the regrettable theory that for the public prints bad news is good news. But the fact is that John Mennons bequeathed to his Glasgow Advertiser and its successors a talent for survival that is virtually unequalled in the trade.

He came to Glasgow to challenge two established newspapers, the Journal and the Mercury, which in their turn had seen off such earlier rivals as the Courant, the Chronicle and the West Country Intelligencer. But the Glasgow Herald, with some small modifications to its masthead, has been in continuous production for two hundred years. It ran indeed almost without a hiccup for nearly 150 years before the General Strike made any serious break in publication – and even then

13

there was a compromise, and as an element in the 'Emergency Press' it appeared every day during the stoppage. With the one exception of the Aberdeen Journal, which dates from the end of the '45 Rebellion, the Glasgow Herald is the oldest national newspaper in the Kingdom, and indeed, in the English-reading world.

To round off the record, it beats The Times by two years, the Dundee Courier by 23 years, and the Scotsman by 33 years. Since 1783, 150 newspapers have been born, waxed and waned in Glasgow. Of these at the time of writing only three survive, the Herald, the Evening Times and the Daily Record.

Who was this John Mennons? He was a printer and an entrepreneur who came into a rapidly growing city and became its leading advertiser. He was personally industrious and had the mettle to face keen competition. His literary quality is a matter of guesswork, for his own hand is visible and identifiable only briefly in the paper, being concerned solely with well-turned, indeed exemplary, announcements of a public relations flavour. There might have been more material upon which to assess his style had he not, when he severed his connection with the paper twenty years later, kept the early bound files to himself; and then lost them. The paper was, in fact, bereft of the natural record of its own beginning for more than a century. A fragile copy of the first issue turned up, squeezed behind the back of a drawer of an old bureau that was auctioned in a Falkirk saleroom. Happily the buyer knew what he found and was generous. Although damaged, it was possible to reconstitute it and seal the sheet between two panes of glass. It was thus possible to make a nearly exact facsimile as an inset to an anniversary number some seventy years ago; and it is from this single relic that we must measure what was John Mennons' initial achievement, and what he aspired to.

The durability of the Glasgow Herald through two centuries of decline and disappearance among its contemporaries may owe something to the realistic tradition which John Mennons sought to establish in the shrewd address with which he introduced his paper to the hard-headed businessmen who were already contemplating, and had indeed initiated, new mercantile enterprises to make good the lost cream of the old American tobacco trade – trade that at its height had seen the Glasgow merchants importing 46,000,000 lb of the weed, and re-exporting most of that. Of these enterprises the most important, and the first of its kind in Europe, was the Glasgow Chamber of Commerce, master-minded by Patrick Colquhoun, and with which the Glasgow Herald shares its bi-centenary.

Here is how John Mennons commended himself as a participator and collaborator in this revival. He allowed himself no extravagant promises, but candidly stated his own self-interest:

In ushering a periodical paper of this sort into the world, the Editor very often informs his readers that his work is to be executed on a plan infinitely superior to that of any other newspaper – that it is undertaken by the particular desire, or under the immediate patronage of independent and most respectable persons – that he has secured authentic intelligence from the very fountainhead of political information – that he is to be favoured with occasional Essays by persons of the highest eminence in the Republic of letters – that he engages in the task of informing and instructing his fellow citizens from the most disinterested motives – and finally that they may have the most entire confidence in his diligence and capacity.

It was a smartly sardonic opening salvo to lead into his own plain, but not unvarnished disclaimer:

The Editor of the Glasgow Advertiser, however, will only say – that his own interest is materially concerned in the success, and consequently in the judicious management of his paper – that he has some experience in the kind of business he has undertaken – that he trusts he can depend on his own industry and labour in the execution of the work – and that he shall preserve his mind as free as possible from any prejudice which, without meaning to impose upon the public, might lead him to partial representation of facts.

He entertains not the smallest doubt of the public candour; and shall be ready to profit by any hint that may be given him for the improvement of his paper.

He then passes the first of his plain compliments upon the foremost commercial city in Scotland and those readers vastly well informed in trade and manufactures, upon whom he is candid to depend for 'any communication on subjects so interesting to the nation in general, and to Glasgow in particular'.

When he wrote this, his first, and so far as the surviving files show, his only leading article, the owner-editor was unaware of the biggest foreign news story that was on its way to him post-haste somewhere between Westminster and the Border. But so far as Glasgow, then and in the future, was concerned, the local story that he did have was of at least equal historic importance.

The late institution of a Chamber of Commerce gives every reason to believe that topics of this kind will occasionally be discussed in such a manner as to lay a foundation for such general and comprehensive conclusions as may serve as guides in critical conjunctures both in the merchant and the manufacturer. The Editor therefor begs leave to congratulate the Public on an institution which promises such good effects, and desirous, as his present undertaking declares him, of connecting his own interest with the interests of this city and the country in its neighbourhood, he cannot be suspected of being insincere in his ardent wishes for their prosperity.

15

Patrick Colquhoun, the father of
Glasgow Chamber of Commerce,
with which
the Herald shares its bi-centenary.

This sanguine conjunction has been sufficiently realised in the Chamber of Commerce's own annual celebration of its antiquity, the Colquhoun Lecture, which is composed and delivered by a member from the relevant year's files of the Glasgow Herald.

It is only honest to report, however, that this was the only bit of Glasgow news to appear in that first number of the Glasgow Advertiser. There were some snippets from Edinburgh, where about three hundred dragoons were standing by to deal with an anticipated mob rising against the price of meal. There was word of a new canal for Borrowstouness; and of a small vessel aground and lost on a rock off Greenock; and there were some echoes of interest by the Gentlemen of the County of Stirling in respect to the representation of the people in Parliament.

The rest was foreign and south-country intelligence lifted from the London Gazette, and the gleanings of letters from several days' post. There were some extracts from the Court Circular, and a couple of columns of Parliamentary report which, in the immediate circumstances, was of interest for the announcement that 'Mr Oswald arrived in town (London) express from Paris with the result of the negotiations for peace. What it is we have not yet been able to discover.' Another absentee from that first number was any word from the 'eminent Correspondent at London' whom John Mennons announced that he had engaged at very considerable expense.

Not then, or indeed for many years, did day-to-day local reporting enjoy much notice in provincial journalism. In this the Advertiser was no different from its fellows. After that opening number, and for the next five years, there are no copies of the paper to go on, but from later issues that have come to light some idea of the contemporary understanding of news value may be taken from the issue for the first week of July 1789, when the total column space amounted to 240 inches. Glasgow got six inches of that, consisting of two obituary notices, and the mention of the death of a boy on shipboard at Irvine from a cruel beating by two of the sailors.

The theory behind this local economy of valuable column inches was no doubt sound enough. In the 1780's, as we can see from John Mennons' own map published in one of his companion enterprises, the Glasgow Magazine and Review, all of the town that mattered was concentrated around the crossing of the only four substantial streets, Trongate, Gallowgate, High Street and Market Street. A later observer made the reasonable excuse that the gossip of the Tontine coffee house and the clash of the women at the well must have been more effective in the diffusion of the latest news of the town and its vicinity than the organs which professed to make this their business. Indeed the Editor of the Advertiser was frank to acknowledge the Tontine, that provincial forerunner of El Vino's in Fleet Street, as the source of most of his own neighbourly intelligence. The imprint on his back page now read:

Glasgow, Printed (every Monday and Friday) by J. Mennons, Tontine Close, Trongate, and sold at his shop, No. 123, the first west from the Exchange, Trongate – where, and at the Bar of the Tontine Coffee Room, Advertisements, Commissions and Articles of Intelligence are taken in.

Trongate and Argyle Street, c 1835

chapter 2

THE RIGHTS OF MAN

The original hand-press on which the first Glasgow Advertiser was printed. It is now in the People's Palace museum on Glasgow Green.

JOHN MENNONS was the son of an Edinburgh journeyman baxter. He was born in the Canongate on 22 February 1747, and learned his printing trade in the caseroom of the Edinburgh Courant. He was going on thirty when he branched out on his own with a printing works in the Lawnmarket, where he set himself up as a maker of almanacs (which remained a sporadic passion for the rest of his life) and established a short-lived Scots and County Magazine.

His first business address in Edinburgh gives a hint of a hitherto unmentioned attraction which he seems to have had to the more out-of-the-ordinary characters of his day. He was acquainted with Deacon Brodie, though he would have been the first to insist that at this time the Deacon was at least superficially respectable. It was an association that was discreetly elided ten years later when the Advertiser reported the execution of that distinguished town-councillor, cabinet-maker and gangster; but for the four years before he came to Glasgow John Mennons ran his

James 'Balloon' Tytler (third from the left) in 1784, at the King's Park, Edinburgh, attempted an ascent in a home-made fire balloon. This pioneer effort (among his many other eccentricities) has been variously reported as a great success and a hilarious failure. Either way it earned him his lasting nickname. The text to this Kay's Portrait credits him with a height of 350 feet. Other authorities assert that he managed only to clear a garden wall before landing in a dunghill.

various and tentative printing enterprises from what was later to be named Brodie's Close in the Lawnmarket.

All the previous biographical notes on the professional life of John Mennons have made much of the assumption, on the evidence contained in his paper, that he was apolitical. But this merely means that he was canny and kept his mouth shut. As one later commentator has it, radical politics could be treasonable besides being unbusinesslike. However, in the light of the only frightening incident that disturbed the first decade of the Advertiser – and indeed marked Mennons' only recorded lapse from caution – it is suggestive to remember that one of his closest collaborators in Edinburgh was James 'Balloon' Tytler, the principal editor of the Encyclopaedia Britannica, an eccentric and random literary genius, with whom he published a periodical called the Mirror, along with the Town and Country Almanack. The significance of that early influence should appear in the sequel.

Mennons, a widower with one son, a modest capital, and a routh of ambition, came to Glasgow to take on the local competition in the winter of 1782. He had £200, a primitive Caxton hand-press – which survives both as a real relic and a pictorial device – and a second- or third-hand fount of well-worn type. He set up shop in an upper flat in Duncan's Land, Gibson's Wynd, off the Saltmarket, where he produced his paper single-handed, and himself carried it damp off the press to distribute along the plainstanes and colonnades at the Cross on the morning of Monday, 27 January 1783.

Diligent in all things concerning his trade, he was equally attentive to the social connections that might commend him, with his unimpressive Edinburgh pedigree, to the consequential social traditions of Glasgow. To that end he set his cap at Jean Steedman, the daughter of a prosperous local cutler, and having married her (in 1785) was admitted a Burgess and Guild Brother of the City. He was thus usefully identified, not only with the bustling Glasgow now seeking to flourish with new enterprises, like the cotton industry, but also with the most diverting and popular folk-lore of the place. This rubbed off on him through his new wife's grandfather, Robin McNair, a grocer, one of Scotland's most cherished eighteenth-century eccentrics and an effective demonstrator, withal, against what he conceived to be official impositions and nuisances.

When the Government put a tax on two-wheeled carriages, McNair took the wheels off his phaeton and fitted it with wooden runners, drawing his biggest and most appreciative crowds when he thus drove his co-operatively self-sacrificing family to church. He was a match for the law, too, particularly in the Exchequer Court, where it was the practice of the Crown, when successful, to reward the jury with their supper and a guinea each.

When McNair himself had a brush with the Exchequer Court – to do with the duty he should have paid on his merchandise – counsel for the Crown included in his address to the jury the reminder that a favourable verdict would bring them the usual reward. At this Robin McNair asked if he, too, might address a word to the jury, and on the judge agreeing he said:

> Gentlemen, you have heard the learned Advocate for the Crown say that he will give you a guinea each and your supper if you bring in a verdict in favour of the Crown. Now here am I, Robert McNair, merchant in Glasgow, standing before you, and *I* promise you two guineas each, and your dinner to boot, with as much wine as you can drink, if you bring in a verdict in my favour.

He won his case; and thereafter, we are told, this was a diet which the Crown deserted.

Accepted into the community, our editor-proprietor did not immediately thrust himself upon it. He was neither clubbable nor very convivial, and he still had his way to make. He was ambitious, and he was diligent; he had to be. There is no record of what he had by way of staff in those first years, if indeed he had any, apart from that insubstantial

'eminent Correspondent at London' who had let him down on his first deadline. The only personal report of the Editor at this time shows him spending his nights back at the office in his carpet slippers, mulling over the London mails and journals, lifting the news, the gossip, and the despatches; and, probably 'stick' in hand, setting up the paragraphs out of his old and limited case of type. It was clearly an application that paid off, for within four years he had moved to more impressive premises at the Tontine Close, 123 Trongate, and was announcing that the Advertiser (and Evening Intelligencer) was now being 'printed with new types cast by Dr Wilson and Sons of this University'. Alexander Wilson was a typefounder of international reputation and would not have come cheap.

At the Tontine Close Mennons lived above the shop, and, indeed, the premises remained in the family for the next hundred years. Never content, as his later life showed, to restrict his expansion, he now had other irons in the fire.

Not only had his paper increased in size to eight pages, and was appearing on Mondays and Fridays, but he was printing directories for his friend, and eventual partner, Benjamin Mathie (a direct descendant of John Knox), clerk to the Trades House, town clerk of Rutherglen, clerk to the Highland Society, and a much respected lawyer and local historian. There were also profitable sidelines in the shop, where there was for a time a brisk trade in lottery tickets and patent medicines.

There soon came a time, however, when his publications and the management of their increasing finances occupied the whole of the founder's attention. By 1797 he could afford to parade his success and for £2435 he bought the peculiar mansion of Jeanfield from his wife's cousin Robert McNair. The house, sitting in seven acres of garden and orchard, near Camlachie, was a creation of Robin McNair, the interesting grocer and distaff relative mentioned earlier, and it bore his hallmark on its 'upwards of 20 apartments besides cellars'. He had built it without the aid of an architect, but with the assistance of a local mason. The place was three-quarters built before either of them noticed that it had no stairs. They had managed, as an afterthought, to erect something like a spiral staircase, but within a year Mennons had had enough of it.

While none of the original bound files has been recovered, there are enough individual papers and collected volumes from about 1788 onwards to give us a fairly comprehensive knowledge of what the paper looked like and how it treated the news.

On the minutiae of the Glasgow scene, the main impression, and that vividly enough, comes from the advertisements; items which in fact entitled the Advertiser in a rudimentary way, to be called a picture paper. There were three small wood-engravings of a horse, a dog, and a cow, which served to draw attention, impartially, to sales, thefts, and strayings of such animals. The horse served in turn as a

The Woodcuts
The paper's first illustrations, and indeed the only ones for a hundred years or more were the basic woodcuts, which, in John Mennons' day, drew attention to the advertisements, mostly the Lost and Found. Many of them, like the cow and the dog, were multi-purpose, but there were specific ones for stage-coaches, shipping, and horse-racing.

brown mare or a bay horse; the dog, as the situation demanded was, to mention but a couple of its many manifestations, 'a Newfoundland answering to the name of Hector' or 'a spotted bitch something of the pointer kind'. The cow, well horned and flop-eared, but with no visible udder, represented all breeds and every sex.

Towards the 1790's, Glasgow did get a separate heading and a column of its own paragraphs mostly of the melancholy kind and there was always good coverage of commercial and shipping news.

Nor was the paper averse from extracting and featuring an intriguing Glasgow angle from the larger foreign, military and Parliamentary scenes that normally monopolised its columns. Take, for example, the French Revolution, which was dealt with faithfully and at sufficiently grisly length. Soon after the guillotining of Louis XVI in January 1793, the Advertiser was able to leaven the darker intelligence with the report that: 'We are credibly informed that Marat in the French Convention is no other person than John White, tambourer, late of Glasgow.'

As for the hard facts, during the last decade-and-a-half of the century the Glasgow Advertiser and Evening Intelligencer kept the Tontine Coffee House, and a respectable few thousands of the reading citizens, more than adequately privy to such sensations as the trials of Warren Hastings, the Presidency and death of George Washington, wars, rumours of wars, the victories of Nelson, and the emergence of Bonaparte. And there was one other matter of moment and private vexation to the Editor and staff of the Advertiser, which, merits a separate notice, since it gave John Mennons, among the eighteen editors of this newspaper, the distinction of being the only one of them to stand in the criminal dock at the Court of Session – and before none other than the fearful Braxfield.

The year 1793 was that of 'The Rights of Man', of Thomas Muir, Younger of Huntershill, and of Robert McQueen, Lord Braxfield, the Judge Jeffreys of Scotland. There was revolution in France, sedition – or at least a hankering after freedom of expression – in Britain, and the Lord Justice Clerk on the bench of the High Court of Justiciary in Edinburgh. There was peril in the air; and John Mennons, non-aligned though he might appear to be, and concerned only with his own pocket and the expanding interests of Glasgow, got himself involved in it.

In the past he has been consistently depicted as the innocent and business-like bystander, whose regard for a gainful advertisement with a news angle clouded for a moment his discretion. This was a discretion which, so far as what appeared in his paper was concerned, has left all subsequent narrators without a clue as to whether he was Whig or Tory. We may, however, be able to find him guilty by association of that more specialised freedom of thought that inspired Braxfield to say to a juryman, passing the Bench on his way to the jury box: 'Come awa' Maister Horner, come awa', and help me tae haang ane o' thae daamned scoondrels.'

In the issue of the week ended 1 February 1793, along with an eye-witness report of the execution of Louis XVI, there appeared in the Glasgow Advertiser the following editorial announcement:

> The Editor's best respects to his numerous subscribers – is sorry to acquaint them, that an advertisement that appeared in his paper of the 23rd November last, from a Society in Partick, has, on investigation by those in authority, been deemed of such a seditious nature as to be the cause of an indictment being served at the instance of his Majesty's Advocate, on James Smith, gunsmith in Gorbals, as the author of the said advertisement, and the Editor as the printer and publisher thereof, in consequence of which they have to appear and stand trial before the Lords of Justiciary in Edinburgh on Monday next, the 4th of February current.
>
> To add to the disagreeable situation of the Editor, his son and two of his principal Compositors have been summoned to appear as evidences in the trial; upon which account as he will have no person remaining behind him in whom he could entrust the management of the newspaper in his absence, he is under the necessity of suspending next publication till Wednesday (when a full account of the business may be expected) and begs his readers will consider that circumstance as a reasonable excuse for adopting such a measure.

He was, however, not so fraught with apprehension as to overlook the opportunity to turn his plight to ingratiating effect by adding the plug:

> The Editor cannot dismiss this article without embracing the opportunity of expressing his gratitude to all his Friends and the Public in general for the very distinguished patronage with which they have hitherto honoured him; humbly solicits the continuance of their countenance and support; and assures them that he is still determined to adhere to that principle of impartiality which should be the characteristic of the Editor of a newspaper.

As for the offending advertisement, it came out of the rising undercurrent for reform that was alarming those, of whom there were plenty in the prosperous side of Glasgow, who believed that 'the constitution was matchless and could not be improved on the face of time'. And when they met to declare this faith they made much of Edmund

Robert McQueen, Lord Braxfield, the 'Judge Jeffries of Scotland' before whom John Mennons appeared, with much better luck than most, during the sedition trials of the days of 'The Rights of Man'.

Burke's thunderous denunciations of the French, the French Revolution, and all its works.

In this immediate case the malcontents were the inhabitants of the adjacent village of Partick who . . .

> Animated with a just indignation at the honour of their town being stained by the erection of a Burkified Society, have formed themselves into an Association under the name of
> THE SONS OF LIBERTY AND THE FRIENDS OF MAN
> At this meeting, from its numbers equally hopeful to the people as formidable to the tools of tyrants, the following resolutions were unanimously adopted:
> 1st.   That this Society do stand forward in defence of the Rights of Man, and co-operate with the respectable assemblage of the Friends of the People in Glasgow, for the glorious purpose of vindicating the native right of Man-Liberty; with a fair, full, free and equal Representation of the People in Parliament.
> 2nd.   That the Sons of Liberty in Partick, having attentively perused the whole works of the immortal author of the Rights of Man, THOMAS PAINE, declare it as their opinion that if nations would adopt the practical use of these works, tyrants and their satellites would vanish like the morning mist before the rising sun – that social comfort and plenty, good order, peace and joy would diffuse their benign influence over the human race.

That was the advertisement; and that, particularly the last paragraph, was the seditious utterance. It was a charge which, exposed to the more tolerant standards of today would have been hard to make stick. But that also was the year when the Lord Justice Clerk was setting his own precedents in the matter of seditions and was telling the more irresolute public prosecutors, 'Let ye just bring me the prisoners, and I'll find ye the law.'

With such a prospect we need not be surprised that the co-defendant James Smith, the agent provocateur from over the river at Gorbals, did not respond to the summons and levanted. Three other signatories of the proclamation, John Auchincloss, John Gibson and Peter Hart, were not pursued. And only the Glasgow Advertiser party, who were hardly in a position to take flight even had they chosen to, turned up before the Lords of Justiciary to thole their assize. No doubt with queasy visions of transportation.

They were lucky. The only final cost of their indiscretion was a two-day delay in the publication of one issue of the paper. It reappeared on Wednesday instead of Monday, with the promised full report and John Mennons had the elusive James Smith to thank for his narrow escape:

> Glasgow, Wednesday, February 6. High Court of Justiciary.
> Monday last came on at Edinburgh the trial of James Smith,

gunsmith in Gorbals of Glasgow and the Editor of this paper; the former indicted and accused at the instance of the Lord Advocate of Scotland for his Majesty's interest, for writing and composing a certain advertisement of a seditious nature, and the latter for publishing the same in his newspaper in the month of November last. Smith having failed to appear, sentence of outlawry was pronounced against him and his bail-bond accordingly forfeited.

The Lord Advocate then arose, and in a very handsome address, told the Court that owing to the elopement of Smith, he proposed to continue the diet against the Editor till Monday se'enight; if by that time Smith was not apprehended (and as he was informed that the Editor was the sole conductor of the Glasgow Advertiser he did not mean, owing to that circumstance, that he should appear at the bar that day unless he received *intimation* to that purpose) he would if he saw proper order the trial to proceed at the next circuit Court of Justiciary to be held at Glasgow.

Happily he never saw proper; and John Mennons, in his apparently ingenuous innocence was never further embarrassed.

If one were to doubt that 'principle of his impartiality' of which he boasted in his first address to his public and find hints of seditious private thoughts, it would be to recall the Editor's close professional association at an impressionable age with the afore-mentioned James Tytler. Tytler was as persuasive as he was erratic. He was a consistent non-conformist with a massive literary and polemical talent. He wrote poetry and history, and produced compilations, eighteenth-century Readers Digests and 'miscellaneous literary work of almost every description'. He wrote essays, and even a treatise on surgery. He published magazines and it was here that he placed his influence on John Mennons. He was, as has been said, editor of the Encyclopaedia Britannica. He was throughout a reformer and proselytiser, and young Mennons sat at his feet.

Tytler wrote tracts for the Friends of the People; and it was just as well that the old association did not crop up during the hearing of the Glasgow Advertiser case, for less than a month before Mennons was summoned to the High Court, Tytler, having gone well over the score with 'A Handbill Addressed to the People', fled the country and was outlawed. He got away to America, where, for the remaining ten years of his life, and in a sympathetic anti-British atmosphere, he ran a newspaper in Salem, Massachusetts.

It is tempting to wonder what the subsequent history of the Glasgow Herald would have been if John Mennons' next journey had not been back to Glasgow but to Botany Bay.

chapter 3

ENTER SAMUEL

AFTER 15 YEARS of single-minded application, and mounting prosperity, the founder grew restless again. He had gone to Glasgow at a time of change, and had risen to the challenge. His paper was double its original size and was appearing twice a week; its circulation was everything that could be expected and the rival journals gave him no anxiety. He had even taken to delegating, and in 1797 he made over one-third of his financial interest in the Advertiser to his eldest son, Thomas. It was not that he was thinking of retiring; he was only turned fifty. He was just beginning to see himself as a captain of industry, and was about to come under the ruinous influence of John Finlayson, one of his wife's cousins and an entrepreneur, who was less than forthcoming about what he had to offer.

Wearying of the oddness and inconveniences of his singular mansion after less than a year, Mennons sold the estate of Jeanfield to Finlayson, who added seven acres to it, and began to dig for coal in what was rumoured to be a rich seam that ran under the estate. He formed the Eastmuir Coal Works Company upon which the newspaper-man began to cast an ambitious eye. It took Mennons a year or two to take the plunge, and in the meantime the development lacked nothing in the good report of its proprietor. In 1802 John Mennons sold his interest in the Glasgow Advertiser to Benjamin Mathie for £900, dipped into the substantial accumulated savings of his twenty years as thriving editor-proprietor; and along with one McCluckie (of whom no more is recorded) took the lease of the Eastmuir colliery, with the promise of its 'five workable seams' of which 'only a part of the upper seam has been wrought'. He also became the owner of 'a good steam engine, two Gins with Ropes and Tubs, several Horses and carts and an excellent Weighing Machine'. He was promised that many superior advantages would attend this work and that the coal was of the best quality. What, however, cousin John Finlayson omitted to say was that the pits were desperately subject to flooding, and that the good steam engine had neither the puff nor the capacity to pump them out.

It is owed to the memory of the man who set the Advertiser/Herald on its salubrious, not to say influential, two hundred years, to round off his career, forlorn tale though it became. In 1804 Mennons tried to dispose of his lease of Eastmuir as a going concern. There were no takers. He carried on for five years, running ever deeper into debt, at last meeting his creditors in the Tontine Tavern, of more prosperous memory. In the meantime he had moved back into his old Tontine property, the 'sometime dwelling and printing office', and was seeking modestly to make ends meet by moving back also into the newspaper and printing business.

Samuel Hunter

There was even an echo of his old flair for introducing a newspaper to its public. There was a paper called the Caledonian, whose partners, in October 1807, decided instead to go into the bookselling and lottery office business. Accordingly its last issue carried the notice that it would cease publication immediately and be replaced by the Western Star which would be published by 'a Society of Gentlemen'. It was printed, and written, by Mennons from his old home, the birthplace of the Advertiser. The leading article, in a recognisable hand, stated that '. . . the proprietors are resolved not to subject themselves to the tax of insincerity by alleging that their paper will be better than any other'. It was in truth no better than the London Gazette to which it owed most of its contents twice a week. Mennons lasted on this paper until 1809, by which time, what with the coal business and the small rewards for his journalism, he was thoroughly bankrupt but still fighting back.

Still in the Tontine Close he began putting out the Glasgow Magazine and Clydesdale Monthly Review – reminiscent of the almanacs of his early Edinburgh days – and advertising it in the Glasgow Herald, now flourishing under the ample overlordship of Samuel Hunter. This lasted two years and, down but still not out, our John was back with the prospectus for his new weekly paper, the Scotsman.

A view of the Broomielaw around 1800, with the kiln of the bottleworks smoking in the background. The kiln of the famous Delftfield pottery works would have been just left of the picture.

Its editorial target was all matters 'philosophic, philanthropic and religious', with special emphasis on Christian missions; in it the reader would find only 'information peculiarly suitable for Saturday evening's perusal'. This was somewhat of a break with his own Glasgow Advertiser tradition, which, if not profane, had always been consistently secular in its approach to the news. This Scotsman survived only until 1813, and disappeared without trace, leaving its title free for the taking when a new newspaper was started in Edinburgh in 1816.

Mennons' attachment to Glasgow as a place to live and work in faded at this time with the death of his wife, and he removed to Irvine, where he set up his printing press once more. It was a family business, with his two surviving sons and his four daughters weighing in to compose and print the Irvine and County of Ayr Miscellany.

He died and was buried there in February 1818; his only sculptured memorial is a footnote upon the headstone, in the High Kirk graveyard in Glasgow, of his son Thomas, who predeceased him by fourteen years.

It is his own fault that John Mennons' literary remains are so fragmentary. That he wrote with assurance and with a good sonorous rhythm is patent in his 'introductions' and in his announcement about about his bit of trouble over the Gorbals gunsmith.

The lack of material upon which to judge him further springs from the fact that while he did keep bound files of his newspaper, he stored them in his house above the shop, which remained in the family when he sold out. He, and his descendants, regarded them as a personal possession, and they were not included in the deal.

Where these files were lost and how they were nearly recovered is a story that belongs to the reign of James Pagan, as Editor, three-quarters of a century later. The precious No. 1 did not turn up until after the centenary of the paper was celebrated. The next earliest, from 1787, is in the Library of Congress at Washington.

There are, however, indications that from time to time John Mennons would turn his hand to poetry – as did at least three other later editors of the Glasgow Herald. And significantly enough there was an essay in his short-lived Glasgow Magazine which might confirm the earlier speculation about sedition. It is an intimate profile of 'Balloon' Tytler, signed by the reversed initials 'MJ', and is unmistakably the work of one who knew the man, and his habits, and approved his outlook.

John Mennons did not concede defeat, and, however unsuccessful at the last, when it came to journalism he knew what he was about. Here are his own last printed words:

> To inculcate virtuous principles and to point out the enormities of vice – to teach by wholesome precept – to draw from the inestimable sources of philosophy whatever may tend to enlighten and instruct, are the duties of those who take upon themselves to add to the stock of General Literature. This is the task which we have imposed upon ourselves.

With his father gone about his coal business, Thomas Mennons plainly had no editorial ambitions, any more than the new senior partner, Benjamin Mathie, who, though he knew that he was on to a good thing, preferred to continue on a profitable basis his old friendly function as legal adviser to the enterprise. And so in the winter of 1802 they scouted around for a third partner, someone with some sort of journalistic experience, who would be invited to buy into the firm for £300. They did not have far to seek. Indeed he came from almost round the corner at 44 Bell Street, and could offer not only a print shop, but an established professional reputation – one perhaps more hilarious than totally respectful, especially among the gossips of the coffee house.

Dr James McNayr had the gift of enthusiasm and self-confidence. Senex was even somewhat understating it when he described him as 'rather a remarkable personage in Glasgow in his day'. And, as much as any amateur, which they all were in those days, he knew something about local newspapers, having been 'projector, establisher and for many years principal conductor of the Glasgow Courier', a journal

How the Herald looked in 1805 – the year of Trafalgar. It first reported the battle with a single column heading: 'Great Naval Victory'.

which had been launched in 1791 and offered some competition to Mennons' Advertiser.

Of his popular days as 'Courier' McNayr we know only that he was – for a time – an infallible weather oracle. His weather forecast had such a habit of being correct that folk actually took it seriously; so much so that when he predicted that Glasgow was about to suffer six weeks of unremitting hard frost, 'this intelligence set all our good folks looking out for their skates, bavaries, dreadnoughts, comfortables, lamb-wool mitts and stockings'.

When these six weeks turned out to be the mildest of the season, without a single night's frost, his attendances at his favourite pothouses became progressively less frequent. He had, however, more all-embracing ideas for his new editorship, and, in the time at his disposal did indeed manage to put some of them into effect. For example he changed the name, and became, therefore, the first Editor of the Glasgow Herald, which appeared with that title on 1 November 1802. The paper's longer pedigree was indicated in the number 1334; but alongside it was No. 1, and this was the figure that became progressive.

It was hardly flattering to the Mennons's, either father or son, that the new Editor introduced himself with the intention to make the Herald 'the equal if not the superior of any paper which has hitherto been published in this city, by establishing a more extensive circulation, obtaining more early and authentic information, and by the insertion of such miscellaneous matter as may occasionally contribute to liven and diversify the too frequently uninteresting, though unavoidable detail of trifling occurrences incidental to a provincial paper'. He also, in his first edition, more than hinted at a sense of values which he expected to commend itself to the businesslike community of his readers: 'The obligations that the Editor has been under to his advertising friends has compelled him to withdraw several articles of political intelligence which he had intended for publication.' This was doubly self-sacrificing, since there is a lingering suspicion that the political intelligence that did appear in subsequent issues under the catchline 'From our London Correspondent' was composed by himself.

He was, however, in a tentative way, the newspaper's first leader-writer. Nothing substantial, mind you, just a few opinionative words of his own added to the end of a news item – a foreign news item, which was generally safer. For example, there was nothing likely to offend Glasgow opinion in the addendum to a paragraph in the second issue of his paper reporting that the Swiss Diet had been dissolved: 'Thus have perished the liberties of Switzerland, a nation which acquired its liberty by its valour, deserved it by its virtue, and for five centuries was respected by the most absolute Powers in Europe.'

The really outstanding thing about James McNayr's editorship, however, was its brevity. He lasted just two months. Maybe he was too stimulating for the more conventional taste of Thomas Mennons and Benjamin Mathie. He was impetuous, probably overbearing, and he was not too good with money; which last was indeed the excuse his partners invoked to get rid of him.

He had the habit of overstretching himself, most memorably when, in an illusory flush of prosperity he decided to build himself a country villa on the heights of Woodlands – where Park Circus is now. Like the

Woodlands, Glasgow – 'McNayr's Folly', and its sale notice in 1805. It was a rather larger house than that occupied by the following Editor, Samuel Hunter.

other eccentric McNair, who was no relative, he had his own notions of layout, and, indeed, of construction. He started by building an ambitious system of outhouses. Then his money began to run out; he scrapped his plans for the villa, and converted the half-finished stables, barns, and coach-houses into a castellated chateau, which has earned its niche in Glasgow Herald folk-lore as McNayr's Folly. What with his folly and the imprudence of his management of the Courier he was bankrupt, and had been since the middle of July 1802, a fact which must have been perfectly well-known to Thomas Mennons and Benjamin Mathie when they chose him as the new editor and partner. Their experience of him in action must have given them second thoughts, for when the time came at the end of December to complete the share transaction, McNayr had not the money and the deal was called off.

The Glasgow Herald of 2 January 1803, contained the announcement that: 'Dr James McNayr, writer, ceases to be concerned in this paper and also as a partner in the printing business carried on by him and the subscribers, Benjamin Mathie and Thos Mennons. While the proprietors have to regret the loss of Dr McNayr as editor, they are exceedingly happy in having it in their power to assure their numerous readers, advertising friends and correspondents that they have formed a connection with a gentleman of considerable literary ability, from whose exertions they trust the public will receive equal satisfaction.'

That was Samuel Hunter.

James McNayr was a capricious man of parts, a native of the town and a product of the old Glasgow Grammar School. He was a member of the Faculty of Procurators, and was the author of 'A System of Conveyancing' and 'A Guide from Glasgow to the Highlands', both books which he himself reviewed warmly and anonymously in the Courier. And why not? After all, only a few years later Walter Scott reviewed 'Ivanhoe', to the tune of about 5000 words, in the Scots Magazine. As for McNayr's LL.D., he was 'the first of our plain citizens who was honoured with that dignified appellation'.

Samuel Hunter was a man of his time – writ large. And, as it turned out, he suited the more relaxed manners and enterprises of the new Glasgow perfectly. He was expansive, any way you looked at him, both in his behaviour and his person; he weighed 18 stones, and had a talent for parade and conviviality which gave both himself and his Glasgow Herald a quizzical popularity that has survived vividly to the eclipse of the fame of successors who were much worthier journalists than he ever pretended to be.

He was, in fact, a splendid choice; although it was an exaggeration that he himself would have dismissed to introduce him to readers of the paper as 'a gentleman of considerable literary ability'. That came later, and was memorable only because it was so excellently idiosyncratic.

Mathie and Mennons, indeed, were taking a chance when they

appointed him. He had been no more successful in his previous business ventures than had Dr McNayr. No doubt it was the engaging personality, for which he is best remembered, that moved the partners, when he could not lay his hands on the £300 for a share in the business, to make the accommodation of letting him owe a large part of it to be paid out of future profits. The gamble paid off all round, and Samuel was in the clear within a few months. Not that he had done anything sensational in the way of changing the image of the paper. It was only gradually that he put his personal touch on it.

The Glasgow Herald and Advertiser still relied upon the London coach to bring the intelligence which found its way into the columns with a minimum of rewriting. But there were now more hands to the plough. The local news, to which he had unlimited and confidential access, he provided himself with the help of his single reporter, one 'Blythe' Jamie McNab, and he even had a 'chief corrector of the press' in the person of Robert Wardlaw, who lent substance and accuracy for more years than even Samuel himself could at last boast. The newspaper was entering the continuing age of cashiers, managers and directors.

At first glance Samuel Hunter's qualifications for his new and incandescent career seem minimal. He was 44 years old and drifting. His only experience was military, and it had not been brilliant; though he did polish that up a bit once he turned himself into the central decoration of the professional, social and civic life of Glasgow.

He was a son of the manse of Stoneykirk in Wigtonshire, and at the age of fourteen he was sent to Glasgow University where he graduated Master of Arts in 1785. Then he turned to medicine, and on qualifying and being admitted to the Faculty of Physicians and Surgeons, he joined the North Lowland Fencibles as a surgeon. He went with them to Ireland for the rebellion of '98, where, finding duty in field dressing-stations unrewarding, he sought and got a fighting commission.

The Fencibles were disbanded in 1800 and he retired with the rank of captain. Back in Glasgow, he made a brief and disastrous incursion into business, buying a partnership in a calendering concern — a business that has to do with rolling and pressing machinery. We do not know what he rolled and pressed, but he did not do it very well, and was painfully straitened when Mennons and Mathie came to his rescue.

From then on he never looked back. He was able not only to develop quite substantial skills as a publicist, but was able also to indulge his military bent in circumstances where he would not escape notice. So, while keeping his eye on the foreign news, and dealing with it faithfully in the four five-column pages of the Herald, now increased in depth and width, he took up arms again in a Glasgow where fear of the French was so urgent that the city raised nine regiments to repel them; one of these was the 4th Regiment of Sharpshooters, with Samuel as major.

Samuel Hunter as seen in a contemporary silhouette

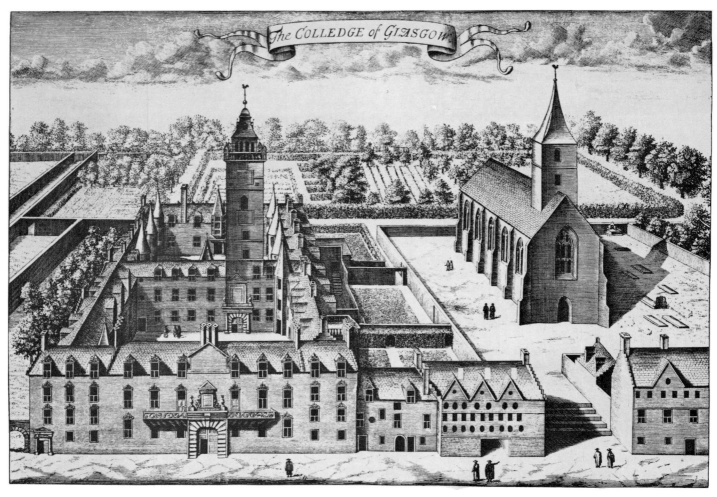

The COLLEDGE of GLASGOW

Glasgow University as it was
when Hunter attended it.

Neither then, nor indeed at any time during the 34 years of his reign,
did the constraints of editing the paper sit heavily on the well-fleshed
shoulders of Samuel. As time went on he wrote more frequently, but
always briefly, and apparently spontaneously; and never to the inter-
ference of the daily perambulations and appearances, either martial or
social, which kept him popular, more than a little unpredictable, and
an irresistable spectacle for the humble citizenry, who could forget
their fear of the French in their enjoyment of watching him, in the full
regimentals that were his abiding vanity, trying to manoeuvre his 18
stones liveweight into the saddle of his charger while parading his
Sharpshooters on the Green.

There were other popular legends, too, about his bulk; notably the
solemn affidavits in such howffs as the Tontine, that on his excursions
to Edinburgh he had to pay double fare to compensate for the amount of
seating space he took up in the coach. He became even more resplen-
dent when, in 1808, the Volunteers were reformed into a militia and he
was promoted Lieutenant-Colonel commanding the 4th Highland
Lanarkshire Regiment, who were handsomely decked in the tartan.

The Colonel's domestic active service lapsed with the abdication of Napoleon, but it enjoyed a gratifying little revival before finally he settled down to an individual line in political commentary, and the consolidating of the warm fortune that his expanding and prosperous newspaper was making for him.

The Radicals, for whom this good Tory never had any time, were on the move again in 1818. Most menacing among them were the weavers; and Glasgow – according to the report of a Parliamentary committee 'one of the places where treasonable practices prevail to the greatest degree' – trembled in the immediate expectation of a rising. Not content with what he could do from his editorial chair, Samuel Hunter, by then a magistrate, presented himself to the Town Council with the offer to recruit the Glasgow Volunteer Sharpshooters, with himself as Colonel-Commander.

The offer was accepted and within a very short time he had a thousand men under arms; but they were called upon only for one night's watch; which they spent sheltering from the rain in St George's Tron Church, while their commanding officer delivered them a pep talk from the pulpit. Indeed for all his military service Samuel Hunter had the good fortune to be wounded only once; and he was out of uniform at the time. During this period of 'absolute trepidation and alarm' in 1819 there was a riot at the haunted house in Queen Street (once the residence of the celebrated 'Bob Dragon') when 'among the gentlemen active for the preservation of the peace on that occasion was the late Mr Samuel Hunter, who received a severe contusion on the head during the riot, which did not end until the dwelling was completely gutted'. The reward for Hunter's Sharpshooters was the official thanks of the Town Council for their 'patriotic zeal and alacrity in the suppression of the late insurrectionary movement'.

St George's Tron Church
in Buchanan Street c 1820.

THE ORACLE OF BELL STREET

chapter 4

SAMUEL HUNTER had the great advantage of being uninhibited by any preconceived editorial conventions. He looked at the news, if there was any, and reacted as naturally as he did when he breezed into his clubs, tap-rooms or military messes, and got into discourse with his peers. He also had the outspoken capacity, in his paper – which soon became a synonym for himself – of getting irritated by the quality of the intelligence that arrived on his desk, and of sharing his feelings with his readers. Thus: 'Our news tonight is altogether of a negative description. There are no further speculations respecting the intentions of the Continental Powers – there have been *no* disturbances in Paris – there are *no* new peers in the Gazette – and *no* new murders in Ireland.'

Nor was he any more tender with his own staff, notably that conveniently anonymous London Correspondent, the artistic verisimilitude of whose existence had been contributing to the journal's influence and consequence ever since the first number of John Mennons' Advertiser. 'Our

Correspondent's letter has been omitted for the unimportance of its contents.' And, 'We have not inserted the Parliamentary paragraph of our Correspondent's letter. There was nothing of interest in it.'

At the same time when the big news did break he did not – at the beginning of his career at least – go out of his way to splash it. While he had taken due note of the war with France and the threat of Napoleon – though more in a practical warlike than in an aggressively editorial way – his first major story was surely the death of Nelson. It was three weeks after the event that he heard of Trafalgar, which he reported briefly in the body of the paper under the single-column heading 'Great Naval Victory'. That was in the issue of 11 November 1805. He fleshed it out in the following weeks, not only giving the fullest report of the public meeting which proposed the monument to Nelson on Glasgow Green, but himself gave three guineas to the subscription, which raised nearly £2000.

Glasgow in the early eighteenth century, with Nelson's Monument

Samuel Hunter played himself in quite cannily. His earlier comments on the news, continuing the McNayr pattern, were short, in his own lusty idiom, but discreetly tailored to avoid offending the local prejudices of his Glasgow readers. Foreigners and foreign affairs were always a popular butt; and it was his felicitous way of cutting these down to size that made 'What's Samuel saying to it to-day?' the catchphrase of the town on his two publication days.

It was not indeed until the closing years of his reign that he chose to sound off deliberately against the tide of current opinion. And that in the end did no harm to his legendary fame. For though his outspoken, and personalised, opposition to the Reform Bill got him burnt in effigy at the Cross – more than once, it is said – he accepted the *fait accompli* with moderately good grace, and he was freely forgiven, for his own jolly sake, and restored to full favour around the Cross where he had recently gone up in flames. In this, as in all the politics of his day, he was consistent. He was a Tory who did not have any taste for change; he would be reconciled to it if it came quietly and slowly; but he pleaded always for 'no interruption to our present state of general courtesy and kindness'. He did not like the Corn Laws; or indeed anything else that in any way annoyed the business interests of the West of Scotland – the expanding urban West, that is. He was humane enough, in an abstract way, about slavery, but he did not take sides in the violent newspaper controversy that raged round the subject in the 1820's, except to concede that it should be abolished eventually.

It was only on Reform that he first grew heated, and he fired some towsy salvos. To begin with he did not want 'to see the electing power disposed among the lesser burghs which share Glasgow's Member, but are unwilling to adopt the full-blown scheme of Whiggery'. When there were disturbances in Edinburgh, which the Scotsman called 'the natural excitement and impatience of the people', he replied, to the applause of his immediate, but reduced, circle of the like-minded: 'Were Edinburgh less gorged by the wealth poured into it from all parts of Scotland, its citizens would not have such a tendency to run rioting.'

He published it as a self-evident truth that 'nobody of the smallest consideration in the West of Scotland supports the Radical cause', and when he lost the match he retired in good order, but with a derisory parting shot at the Liberal press, which 'has taken up the notion that it carries through the Reform measure. It is the fly on the wheel.' Adding, with a realism that might just have been hindsight, that in any case the newspapers could hardly have affected the course of events. After a short lapse, which worried William Dun, the cashier, more than it did the Editor, the circulation picked up again.

Although he did not live to see – and deplore – the Disruption, Samuel, with his rollicking antipathy to zealots and 'Godless radicals', was able to discharge some of his more resonant thunderflashes during the early confrontations in the Ten Years Conflict. The inspiration of his displeasure was the Veto Act of 1834 by which the General Assembly of the Church of Scotland signalled the end of 'patronage'. The burden of the Act was that no minister could be 'intruded' on any congregation contrary to the will of the parishioners, and that if the majority of the male heads of families were opposed to any presentee, this would be conclusive against him 'whether such dissent shall be expressed with or without the assignment of reasons'.

Hear Hunter on this affront to the Establishment: 'Be the patron king or subject, he cannot now count upon his right, unless under the sufferance of the parishioners, many of whom will be passive followers of some busy, intermeddling juncto. And prospective ministers will be exposed to the doubtful result of a humiliating canvass.'

On the earlier debated subject of Catholic Emancipation Samuel

Hunter had been, if not liberal, at least fairly easy-going, except that he was less than sentimental about Ireland and enjoyed a gamesome aversion to Daniel O'Connell, whom he clearly had in mind when he wrote: 'Ireland is a spoiled country, and her orators are so many blubbering boys, who will want for nothing that wailing with a dash of bullying will obtain.'

One *cause célèbre* which the Glasgow Herald treated with the greatest circumspection was the affair of the Queen Caroline Divorce Bill. Her most vociferous local defender was the garrulous chronicler Peter Mackenzie, whose brimming affection for the Editor (who had been his commanding officer in the Sharpshooters) was sorely tried by the fact that: 'While almost every town and city of any note in the Empire were moving in this matter, and transmitting to her Majesty their addresses of warm sympathy and support, the great city of Glasgow was alone remaining mute, or apparently silent and passive.' The Magistrates (of whom Samuel Hunter was one), as was well-known, were perfectly frantic in favour of the King, and few dared publicly to attempt to thwart or oppose them.

It must be said for the paper that it did not miss much, though it had a reassuring composure while waiting for the news to filter north. There was for example the unhurried matter of Waterloo. Glasgow was

Glasgow from Knox's Monument

apprised of it piecemeal, and without any typographical fuss. The battle was completed on Sunday, 18 June 1815, and Nathan Rothschild was already half way to London, not, however, to spread the news but to buy up the stock that was to net him his first million. In the circumstances it would be unfair to chide the Glasgow Herald that in its edition of Monday, 19 June, all it was able to report was that 'a gentleman newly arrived from the Netherlands' had passed on a rumour that an engagement was expected soon.

Friday's issue caught up, but briefly, when a small despatch well buried, and headed only 'Flanders Mail', reported that the Duke of Wellington had announced a victory.

Monday's paper had two headlines:

GLORIOUS AND DECISIVE VICTORY
LONDON GAZETTE EXTRAORDINARY

The story, without involving any make-up or special display, gave details of the engagement and announced the abdication of Napoleon. The delay had its advantages, for the public, having been granted the better part of a week's anticipation, doubled the circulation of the issue of the 26th to some 2000 copies.

Whatever the standard of reporting, which seems to have been adequate, with emphasis on Parliamentary debate, and an increasing attention to local news, Samuel Hunter certainly brightened his paper, and remained impartially critical of the intelligence, on bad as well as good days. 'For the few reports which at present are the only substitute for authentic news, we refer to our private correspondence, and to the paragraphs under the London head of Friday. Long may we continue in this barren state. To show the very destitute condition of the periodical press we shall quote a leader from the London Courier of Thursday: "We have just now received Dutch papers to the 5th instant. They state that the Duke of Saxe Weimar has had a fall from his horse, and *broken* ONE *of his ribs*."'

He had no occasion, however, to be diffident about his excellent report of what we imagine was the last fatal duel in Scotland, which was fought at Auchtertool in Fife, when Alexander Boswell of Auchinleck, the son of Johnson's gossip, received a ball in the neck from the pistol of James Stuart, Younger, of Dunearn, and died the next day. There was a newspaper angle to the challenge, but one which gave the Herald the satisfaction of being the blameless observer. Stuart, an ardent Whig, had been lampooned in its local competitor, the Sentinel; and when Boswell was identified as the author and refused to apologise, he was called out. Stuart was charged with murder in the High Court – and the jury acquitted him without retiring.

Samuel was eminently sociable and extrovert. His compeers generally shared his opinions and relished his conversation. This cannot be said, however, of some of his more demure successors on the paper when they came to celebrate in print some of its earlier anniversaries. Round the turn of the century, for example, we find him faintly praised with the reproof: 'The examples of his wit that have come down to us have about them a distinctly Scottish tang, as well as a robustness that makes an imperfect appeal to the present day sense of refinement.' And if that is not more than a hint that he was a verbal libertine and spreader of unprintable saws, what about this, which graced the paper's columns as recently as 1933? 'It is difficult to have wit accepted on trust, and it is to be feared that most of the sallies with which Samuel Hunter is credited by tradition are of a coarseness and candour that would not now be tolerated.'

He deserves a modicum of rehabilitation, for these prim strictures have their source in a single 'unprintable' anecdote that has come down by word of mouth. When he was Commander of the 4th Highland Lanarkshire Regiment, whose full Highland dress was the talk of the town, and not least the splendour of the 18-stone Colonel, it was reported to him that someone had asked how many yards of the tartan it had taken to make him his kilt; to which he replied, to the uproarious delight of the coffee house: 'Ask my erse.'

The Editor of the Glasgow Herald certainly partook of all the diversions of his age, and it does him less than justice to make such a harmless aside the foundation of a reputation for unseemliness. There is no doubt that his repertoire would have included some even broader impurities, but in public he was generally as discreet as he was jocose, and it is a fair guess that he reserved these for the more exclusive intercourse of his club, where such pleasantries enjoyed a freedom which may already have been eroding a little under the influence of Mrs Grundy. He was an enthusiastic member of the Hodge Podge Club, a brotherhood which has been chronicled with endearing ambiguity, and probably innocence, by Dr John Strang, the mid-Victorian City Chamberlain and historian of the Glasgow clubs.

The original choice spirits were the Tobacco Barons, who put it about that they met to discuss literary and political matters and to play a little whist. They dined at nine once a fortnight; and by the time that he became their brightest ornament, they were saying of Samuel (for outside consumption) that he was the Solon of their club, and that 'his political prophecies were as attentively listened to and as religiously believed as those of his ancient and illustrious namesake'. In fact their meetings were lustier fun than that. And, though lacking perhaps some of the more arcane rituals, they shared the well-recorded tastes of the merry Monks of Medmenham – inaccurately known to notoriety as the Hell-Fire Club.

The entertainment, lubricated with claret and enlivened by the imaginative management of the wagers book, had that circumspect permissiveness that was considered perfectly all right for public men of the eighteenth and early nineteenth centuries. After all, Francis Dashwood, Baron le Despenser, and the leading celebrant at the rites of St Francis of Wycombe, was Chancellor of the Exchequer; and he numbered persons of the like and fame of John Wilkes among his cronies. Both these fraternities had transient female members. The only difference was that at Medmenham they were called 'Nuns', while the Hodge Podge in its transactions merely listed them as the 'belles to be the standing toasts for the twelvemonth'.

The Hodge Podge – named for the oatmeal dumpling which became but the token delicacy at their board – had its own monosyllabic loyal toast; but this was a toast proclaiming a very particular, unconstitutional devotion. And its treasures, notably the insignium of office of the preses, were singular. The minutes of the club, meticulously kept, were so skilfully composed that, like Thomas Bowdler's Shakespeare, they could be read by the uninitiated and not 'raise a blush on the cheek of modest innocence, nor plant a pang in the heart of the devout Christian'.

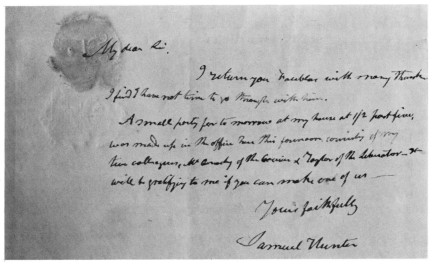

The standard quotable anecdote about Samuel conflicts a little with the general report that his wit was without malice. One of the early partners, the successor, in fact, to Thomas Mennons (who died in 1804) was Dr William Dunlop, a surgeon of some local reputation, but not so tied to his profession as to prevent his taking what Samuel Hunter interpreted as too diligent an interest in the business affairs of the paper. They did not see eye to eye; a situation that has never been uncommon in newspapers between the editorial department and the counting house. One night, when our man was out of town, fire broke out at 77 Bell Street. Dunlop was there, though; and, despite his age and delicate health (he died the next year), he climbed on to the blazing roof carrying buckets of water, which he spilt. He slipped from the ridge, and only by catching his feet in the gutter did he escape falling into the street. The Editor's only comment, when this was reported to him the next day was: 'Aye, I daur say. Thae rhones kep a heap o' trash.'

Appropriately, it is as a footnote to the Hodge Podge Club that we find the most comprehensive if partial assessment of the man who ran the paper and held the quizzical attention of the town for 34 years. Here is Dr Strang again: 'He became a favourite with the best society in the City, not more for his wit and good humour than for his innate principles of honour and gentlemanly deportment. . . . He was the caressed and respected of all. . . . Mr Hunter was possessed of an enlarged and cultivated mind, but his distinguishing quality was sterling sound sense. His style of writing was terse, clear, and occasionally epigrammatic. Affectation and conceit to him were an abomination, and in spite of his constant good nature he was sometimes tempted to pour out a vial of pungent satire on those who exhibited either of those disgusting peculiarities. . . . A man of high honour, true patriotism, of considerable learning, of sound sense and of unostentatious benevolence. . . . As a guide and controller of public opinion in the west of Scotland he was regarded as little less than an oracle.'

He retired in 1836 and died at Kilwinning, in the manse of his minister nephew, on 9 June 1839.

Almost continuously during the 34 years of Samuel Hunter's caliphate, there was a fluctuating intrusion of outside financial interest into the paper. To be fair it was not all that 'outside', since the investors were mostly local worthies who when need be were more than willing to take a hand in the running of the show. First among these was William Dunlop, already mentioned, an 'able and ingenious' surgeon and the first to deliver clinical lectures in the Glasgow Infirmary. He had taken over the original family shares when Thomas Mennons (the son of the founder) died in 1804, and regarded himself as business-manager of the enterprise. Then there was Robert Wardlaw, the proof reader and Samuel's only editorial assistant, whose father had worked for the old Advertiser. When Dunlop died in 1809, Wardlaw and Samuel Hunter divided his shares between them.

Meanwhile Benjamin Mathie was still in the offing, keeping his

Glasgow Infirmary, with Barony Church on the right

Samuel Hunter's house at the corner of Montrose Street and George Street – only a stone's throw from the Herald's present building.

legal eye on the books, as he would for the next quarter of a century. In this matter he did not need to be all that vigilant, for in the interim William Dun had joined the staff in 1811. He was probably the canniest man that ever passed through the Herald's counting house, and by the end of the day, which was still a long way off, he had done equally well for the company and for himself.

Dun was the cashier – and eventually manager and partner – and he knew exactly where the pennies came from and went, for he kept them exactly under his own hand. It is perhaps a measure of the law-abiding streets of Glasgow that he carried the company's cash about with him in his pockets, the notes and sovereigns in one, and the lesser coins made up into packets of £1 each in another. From this personal till, in office, street or tavern, he paid the accounts to the creditors and the wages to the printers. He took his business with a gravity and assiduity that excluded him from the extrovert social life of his editor; he lived in modest bachelorhood in lodgings above a bakery in Union Street, aspiring to some grandeur too late in his pilgrimage to have the enjoyment of the fortune that he had accumulated. He outlived both Samuel Hunter and his successor George Outram; and in 1860 he bought the estate of Craigton and Culcreuth, near his native Fintry (where his father had been the miller). There he set about building a mansion and a mausoleum. He died in 1861.

He saw – and clearly had a decisive hand in making – the paper prosper; and he acquired a more profitable interest in its progress when on the death of Benjamin Mathie in 1831 he and Hunter divided that old partner's shares between them. This share-dealing, then as

44

now, must have been of more interest to the various partners than to the multiplying company of readers; but it has the importance that it had an influence upon the editorial succession.

On the death of Mathie, the role of personal legal adviser to the Editor was assumed by Alexander Morrison, among other distinctions Dean of Faculty and Commissioner of Police. When Samuel's health began failing in 1835 he sold out to Morrison and Dun, and it was these two, along with the aged Wardlaw, who were faced with the task, a thankless one as it turned out, of finding a new editor.

Samuel Hunter had been engaged to edit the paper at £60 a year. As reward for his early promise this was soon increased to £80, and then to £100, which remained his salary for upwards of thirty years. This, however is not to suggest that he was exploited. He shared so hand-somely in the profits that his average income over a significant period of years was £1077. And even at the end he did not all that badly, for just before he retired in 1836 he collected his share of that year's profit, amounting to £1800; he then unloaded his shares to his partners for £8000.

During this period, and indeed for some time after, the practical impediments to an expanding Glasgow Herald were the double Government impositions of Stamp Duty and Advertisement Tax. The selling price had to be 7d to accommodate a duty of first 3½d and then 4d on every copy. But they coped. Samuel made a promise that he would stand his staff and friends a slap-up party the day when there were more than a hundred advertisements in the Herald. About the middle of his term he kept that promise – even if he did not take his guests to taste the delights of the Hodge Podge.

In 1809 the annual profit was £800; in 1836 it was £3600. And the pursuit of circulation and advertising revenue was not made any easier by the levy of 3s 6d that was laid on every advertising insertion. There was a brief prospect of relief in 1833 when this tax was reduced to 1s 6d. But there was a nasty surprise in the small print. This came under the heading of 'Separate Interests'.

Here is the heartfelt complaint of a counting-house manager, Alex-ander Sinclair, who had to deal with it into the next generation: 'When pricing the advertisements we had to read them carefully in case there might appear in any one of them the semblance of the interest of more than one person; because if, for instance, an advertisement referred to more than one property for sale, which belonged to more than one person, the Government would certainly charge us 1s 6d for each owner. When adjusting our accounts monthly with the sharp-eyed official I had many a tussle as to what was more than "one interest" – a phrase which occasionally appeared at the end of an advertisement so as to anticipate the official's challenge. But we had occasional trouble also in persuading advertisers that, as we would be charged for more than one, we required to charge them accordingly. On one oc-casion an old house-factor was in this position: as he would not admit

that he saw the reason why, I gave him a personal illustration by saying that if he and another man each wanted a wife, and stated their wants in one advertisement it would mean four interests. He paid down without another word for two interests; but I did not learn till after he had gone that I was innocently more apt and personal than I had intended, as it turned out that he had recently got his discharge from one wife and was trying to annex another.'

The title of the paper underwent some, but unimportant, changes. In 1803 it was Herald and Advertiser and Commercial Chronicle; which was so patently cumbersome that it lasted only a few months to be replaced on Monday, 26 August 1804 by Glasgow Herald. The definite article appeared once more in 1834.

Though the circulation rose to some 2500 copies an issue there were no very great improvements made in the machinery that produced the paper. True the old Caxton press had been changed, but only to a Columbian Press, not radically different in design, and capable in the hand of two hard-wrought first-class men, of turning out some 350 impressions an hour. There were from time to time changes in the size of the paper, which while staying at four pages, saw these increased in width to accommodate six, and then seven columns; and in length to 24 inches.

With Hunter gone, the three partners for no reason we can guess at this distance, decided that the next Editor would be Francis Weir, of whom no more is known than that he was a graduate of Aberdeen University, and was hired at a salary of £300 a year. But when it came to the bit he pleased them no more than James McNayr had contented their predecessors. He lasted for only a few weeks, was removed from office and lingered, apparently paid but idle, until the last we see of him is the word 'stopt' against his name in the wages ledger for June 1837. In the meantime the junior partner and aged corrector of the press, Robert Wardlaw, being the only remaining person who knew how to do it, reluctantly took over the running of the paper, until they could find a new editor; who was George Outram.

Columbian Press
of the early nineteenth century.

chapter 5

A SLIGHTLY BIBULOUS FLITTING

NEITHER his most ardent admirer, nor indeed his worst enemy – if such a cheerless caitiff were to be imagined – could have said of Samuel Hunter that he was refined or cultivated in the Athenian style. One must just wonder what it was that moved the three partners, thirled as they were to the huckster and uncompromisingly mercantile mood of the west of Scotland, to decide what the Glasgow Herald now needed was the mildly Attic wit of the dilettante George Outram.

Not that it was an error of judgment. Just that it was odd. He sat as Editor for nineteen years, and it is hard on his memory and his talent that while plenty happened in that time, both to the country and in the paper, his principal achievement might seem to be simply that he became eponymous. George Outram and Co. survive, 145 years on; and yet the most that Glasgow chooses to remember of him is that he wrote light verse. Admittedly he was not the most aggressive of newspaper tycoons, but he was the most cultivated editor of his generation and he was putting his influence on a

George Outram

quality journal at a time when, politically and socially, the Herald's London contemporaries were more notorious than respected. He never bludgeoned Glasgow but rather caressed it with a subtler persuasion, which paid off even when he took an unpopular line on the question of Free Trade.

He was reserved and shy, and private; and was, in fact the perfect counterpoint to his only editorial assistant, James Pagan – who as the first professional journalist, himself as Editor eventually became the most important person in the Herald's editorial development. It was George Outram's habitual moderation that gave useful point and surprise to his occasional indulgence in more acid rebuke where he thought it was deserved. Even in the crisis of the Disruption, while sticking to the Establishment guns, he avoided the harsher words and was more propitiatory than Hunter had been at the beginning of the Ten Years Conflict. He had extreme reservations about the Declaration of Spiritual Independence, which asserted: 'In all matters touching the doctrine, government, and discipline of the Church, her juridicatures possess an exclusive jurisdiction founded on the Word of God.'

But when Dr Chalmers led his cohort of free and protesting ministers from St Andrew's Church, through the streets of Edinburgh to their new Assembly at Tanfield Hall, then Outram, declaring again his affection for the Establishment, 'never doubted nor disparaged the motives of the seceders'.

George Outram was an advocate, and an Edinburgh one at that. And one who during ten years of unenthusiastic professional attendance learned that he had not the bounce or the aggression to make much of a way in the strutting competition of the sculptured concourse of Parliament House. He was an observer of his fellows rather than a participant in litigious logomachies. It was for his private satisfaction that he set down his judgment in verse in the 'Legal Lyrics' which, while for many years they diverted his intimate friends, who even set them to music, were not published until after his death.

As Editor of the Herald his concern was to 'prevent innovation on our venerable and cherished institutions'; though on occasion he was prepared to compromise his preference for the status quo. He was, for example, one of the early Scottish nationalists, and a member of the National Association for the Vindication of Scottish Rights Movement, which was doing rather well until it was overtaken and defused by the outbreak of the Crimean War. The complaint, which remains unmitigated to this day among the like-minded, was that the promised privileges of the Treaty of Union had not been implemented. The members mourned the loss of our Privy Council and other Courts; condemned the 'degradation of the heraldic emblems to subordinate place on the Royal Standard'; and demanded the revival of the Scottish Household with the title of Prince Royal of Scotland for the heir to the Throne. The Herald's contribution to the campaign was the injunction

Queen Victoria and Prince Albert on visit to Glasgow in 1849. They arrived on the yacht 'Fairy' and later travelled by rail to Balmoral.

that, 'Any man calling himself a Scotsman should enrol in the National Association.' George Outram himself made a rare excursion from his chosen seclusion to join the Earl of Eglinton on the platform at a mass meeting in Glasgow.

On this matter the Scotsman was tepid, and laid itself open to the Herald's counter-charge of lacking patriotism. Indeed it was about this time around the early 1850's that the Herald found in itself a revived taste for cross-country slanging which had declined under the benign influence of the newly-appointed Outram. It started with the Scotsman's tendentious extrapolation of a Parliamentary report of a 21-year survey of drunkenness in big cities; which according to the Edinburgh journal 'stated positively every twenty-second person in Glasgow is taken once a year drunk to the police office. Stated comparatively, Glasgow is three times more drunken than Edinburgh . . .

49

and is at once the Presbyterian Rome and the modern Gomorrah.' Outram responded shrewdly and sharply with counter-charges about the self-deluding way in which Edinburgh kept its own drunken statistics.

This interlude is, however, of principal interest in pointing the well-mannered restraint that had for too long replaced the boisterous flamboyance of Samuel Hunter. Indeed seemliness had been so overweening that the Glasgow Examiner, an evanescent local rival, hailed the Herald's re-entry into controversy with this left-handed compliment: 'All persons will be delighted, and many surprised, at seeing our old friend across the way so croose on this subject. Many thought that good living and downie repose had superinduced such a taste of constitutional numbness as to prevent for ever his dander getting up unless at the French. He has laid about himself so lustily that the Goliath of the east begins to put on wry faces and protest he was only in fun.'

Our gentle editor was born in 1805 when his father was manager of the Clydebridge Ironworks; and George seems to have been the first maverick in a family of engineers. His uncle was Benjamin Outram, the civil engineer who in 1800 was the first to introduce iron railways for the colliery traffic in the north of England. These tracks through the galleries, adits and landing stages of the mines were called Outram roads, which made it inevitable that a few years later an expert would write '. . . and this by an easy abbreviation was changed to *tramroads*, a name that has lived ever since'. Which may be irrelevant unless we cite it for George as an Outram tradition of keeping their enterprises on the rails. Certainly under his direction the paper enjoyed a couple of decades of great tranquillity.

The Glasgow Herald was little disturbed when in 1847 the North British Daily Mail was launched; a threat to which the perfectly self-confident response was to add Wednesday to the Monday and Friday which till then had been the publishing days; though this had an aftermath a few years later in the time of James Pagan.

As has been said, George Outram is better remembered as a lyricist than as a campaigning journalist. What indeed, are we to make of his own paper which, when he died after a lingering frailty in 1856, mourned the passing of a lamented friend, lauded the gentle wit that refreshed, delighted and instructed all who were privileged with his friendship, examined the 'blended pathos, wit and humour and true poetic fire of his composition which, modestly, he hardly spoke of as his own'; and yet so far as his twenty years of editorial management were concerned, could find the inspiration only to write: 'It is not for us to speak of the manner in which Mr Outram performed the important functions committed to his charge; but this we know that his was the soul of honour, truth and candour, and these, the distinguishing features of his own mind, it was his study to impress upon the journal.'?

We get a better impression of his editorial quality from another more

A Glasgow crowd is dispersed during the Bread Riots of 1848. The control of grain prices as a result of the Corn Laws often brought suffering to the poor.

Spreull's Court, 114 Trongate –
one of the many places the Herald's
caravan has rested. In the eighteenth
and early nineteenth centuries the
business life of the city
was centred around the Tron.

specific epitaph: 'He loved what was old and pleasant and easy, and shrank with a sort of humorous abhorrence from what was obtrusive, either in social or political life.'

George Outram was undoubtedly indolent, an aesthetic imperfection which one would be generous to attribute to the delicate health which dogged all his days, and made the last years of office little more than mere semi-retirement. But he was fortunate in having about him men who were vigorous and eager. On the business side there were Dun and Morrison and then Alexander Sinclair who stayed with, and subsequently managed, the paper for fifty years. And, of course, editorially there was James Pagan.

Outram was the assenting observer rather that the instigator of the decisions and physical changes steady progress was imposing on the Glasgow Herald. The first of these changes, made almost immediately after his appointment, was the flitting from Bell Street to the 'more commodious premises' in the first-floor back of Old Post Office Court in Trongate. We do not know how much more commodious; only its exceptional neighbourly amenities have come down to us. The Herald here was sandwiched between a synagogue on the upper floor and a public house at ground level; and there is no doubt which was the better frequented. We have it on the authority of the chief reporter that: 'It is worth mentioning that out of gratitude for the great addition which was made to the business of the public house, the landlord conceded to all the workmen belonging to the Herald the privilege of getting their whisky a penny a gill below the market price.'

This, however, was a perquisite that lasted only three years, until 1840, when the purchase of a bigger printing press dictated the removal, still in Trongate, to a former Methodist Chapel in Spreull's Court. This was a substantial building put up by an eighteenth-century City Chamberlain, and originally used as a muslin warehouse. The printing was done in a cellar below the counting house, and the press was only a marginal mechanical advance upon the Cowper, a Manchester artifact, worked by 'three strong labourers who turned a wheel like that of an immense grindstone; and terrible work it was – two always groaning and sweating while a third rested'. At their maximum productivity they were able to run off about 750 sheets an hour, printed on one side. That made an output of some 350 four-page papers an hour, after turning over, pulling again, and folding.

The next improvement, again one in which George Outram had little say, was the introduction in 1851 of two cylinder machines built by Brown of Kirkcaldy, and capable of turning out a thousand papers an hour. These were efficient enough, but were a constant source of anxiety to the watching printers, and to the occasional onlooker from the editorial department; for they (to quote a reminiscent Pagan, who lived to see electric eight-feeder rotary machines, printing twenty thousand sheets an hour) were driven by 'the most frantic little steam engine I ever beheld, for, when at work, it tumbled eternally from one side to the oher, as if it was making an incessant effort to turn itself upside down, and never could succeed'.

George Outram had been taken on at a salary of £400 a year – Samuel Hunter's for the better part of 30 years had been £100; inflation is not a peculiarity of our time. But that was just the beginning. Within a few months he was made a partner. The holding of the company, to which he immediately gave his name, consisted of 28 shares of a nominal value of £100 each. These, after the death of Robert Wardlaw, were distributed as follows: William Dun, 19; Alexander Morrison, 4; George Outram, 4; and David Waters (a brother-in-law of Dun), 1. In the course of this editorship there were other transactions, and additional shareholders, including James Coltart, another of William Dun's relatives, who succeeded him as manager when he decided to take it, if not easy, at least easier, after 35 years of daily attendance at the Glasgow Herald counting house. The significance of these shares as an indicator of how well the paper was doing is to be seen in a deal that was concluded towards the end of Outram's nominal editorship. In 1854, two years before his death, he was conceding that Pagan, his sole assistant, had assumed full editorial responsibility. Alexander Morrison, with George Outram's connivance, decided that it would be farsighted to sell one of his shares to Pagan. This he did; and the asking price for this single nominal £100 share was £2750. With the assistance of George Outram and a couple of other friends, plus £500 of his own savings, James Pagan met the price and joined the firm.

George Outram saw the circulation of the Glasgow Herald swell to 4500 an issue, and in that connection was party to one of its more diverting public controversies; the paper's Parthian shot, although untypically rough, was sufficiently Olympian to have been loaded and fired by himself. This was just before the final abandonment of the Stamp Duty; and at that time the official annual return of stamps issued to newspapers was the accepted way of calculating and recording their circulations.

One of the Herald's Glasgow contemporaries, though hardly a rival, was the Mercantile Advertiser. Its editor and proprietor accused the Herald of administering an intolerable slight and, with unintentional but well-grounded flattery, used our own advertising columns in order to give his complaint the widest possible circulation.

On Monday, 10 April 1854, the Herald had published in tabular form the Parliamentary return of the number of newspaper stamps issued to Glasgow newspapers for the years 1851, 1852 and 1853. The Mercantile Advertiser took its place at the bottom of the list with no stamps for 1851, 3500 for 1852 and 12,000 for 1853. A second table showed average circulation for each number, calculated from the number of stamps supplied. There were 16 papers on the list, on which the Herald came near the top with an average circulation of 4500, and the Mercantile Advertiser last – with 241.

The advertisement, in the next issue of the Herald, which came out on the Friday, was headed in bold type:

MISREPRESENTATIONS OF THE GLASGOW HERALD

and set out in round terms that the statement of the circulation of the Mercantile Advertiser had been entirely FALSE.

> . . . . The circulation of this journal – distinguished during the past five years as the leading unstamped paper in Scotland – does not, of course appear in the return except for the number of stamps used for that portion of our impression sent by post.
>
> . . . . Our city circulation in places of business *free from the Government stamp* is well known to be unequalled and unapproached by any of the political newspapers.
>
> . . . . The 'Herald' has the audacity to state our average circulation as 241, well knowing these figures to represent only a small fraction of our issue. It will gain nothing by this cowardly and disgraceful attempt to injure us – the falsehood is too glaring to be believed.

Outram, properly incited no doubt, did not suffer such squibs gladly, but dealt with the advertisement editorially and derisively, thus:

> If the man is displeased with his circulation, he must blame facts and figures – not us. Would he have been better pleased to have been left out of the return altogether? We observe, however, that the 'Mercantile Advertiser' tries to get out of the difficulty of an attenuated circulation by designating himself 'the leading unstamped paper in Scotland'. This leads us to ask what are the grounds on which he enjoys an exemption from the penny stamp? We see pretty plainly, however, through the motives which have directed this publication. Had the owner of the 'Mercantile

Advertiser' confined his malignity and mendacity to his own columns they would have been unnoticed and innocuous so far as we are concerned; for we know so little of his journal that until some 48 hours ago we were not even acquainted with the day of the week on which it usually sees the light – a measure of ignorance which we believe to be shared with 99 out of every 100 of the population.

At this point the writer wearied of the whole business and concluded: 'But we cannot waste more time and space on a person of this sort. We spit upon the creature and bid it gone.'

And that seems to be a sufficiently towsy last word to leave with the gentle George Outram.

Shipping on the Clyde at Broomielaw, c 1835

chapter 6

THE DAILY PAPER

THE EARLY EDITORS of the Glasgow Herald – most of them also proprietors – were an almanac-maker, an aspiring coal baron, an eccentric weather forecaster, a bon-viveur and enthusiastic Home Guard, an unknown from Aberdeen, and a poetic advocate from Edinburgh. Under their amateur, but receptive, direction the paper developed and flourished, extending its commercial importance in the West of Scotland, and promoting its own brand of Tory independence. It increased in size and multiplied its advertisements, and made, for its generation, handsome profits in what was then, as it has always been, a fiercely competitive enterprise. There were some advances in machinery, and two or three transfers to 'more commodious premises'.

That says much for the amateur, for it was not until 73 years after the foundation of the paper that the first professional journalist was appointed, or in this case promoted, to the editorial chair. He was James Pagan, and he was a reporter. His appointment was inevitable. He had, in fact, been on the staff of the Herald for 18 of the twenty years that Outram was Editor; during that time, certainly the latter half of it, his had been the dominant influence upon its news gathering, its policy and its production. For most of that time, too, he was all the staff; his own recollection being that 'the editorial and reporting departments were exclusively filled by the late lamented George Outram and myself. We had not a correspondent in the kingdom to whom we had a right to look for a scrap of intelligence.'

He was, from the start, an innovator, especially in the matter of getting the Scottish news, and not only reporting it fully but seeing to it that his copy reached the printer the same day; a detail which till then had not much interested the local editors, nor indeed the public, which only now began to learn for the first time that it might not be necessary to wait until Friday to read what had happened, or been said, the previous weekend.

His first demonstration of his Pony Express, or fast relay, technique came with what was probably his first out-of-town assignment when in the summer of 1839 he was sent to Ayr to cover Eglinton Tournament. That was the magnificent and romantic assault-at-arms, carried out in what he took to be the ancient style by the 15th Earl of Eglinton, with knights in armour (among them Prince Louis Bonaparte, afterwards Napoleon III), and a presiding Queen of Beauty in the person of the Duchess of Somerset. This was a noble frolic which was expected to cost £2000, but the total bill worked out at £40,000. Not only did Pagan make the most of the spectacle and turn in a fine descriptive reporting job, but he laid on a system of staged despatch riders to get his copy to Glasgow post-haste – and deadlines ahead of the reporters from the four or five other Glasgow papers. Here is his own description of the operation: 'There were neither railways nor telegraphs in those days, but, by way of doing a tremendous bit of *expressing* at this tournament, Mr David Waters, the principal clerk, came out to Irvine on the coach; he waited till my report of the first day's proceedings was written out, started on foot, and in the dark, between three and four in the morning, made his way to Johnstone, where he got the track boat, and got into Glasgow in the forenoon, where the matter was comfortably put in type for the next day's paper.' Pagan was also the 'first in Scotland to develop a wider field for the pencil of the shorthand-writer', having himself practised to get the speeches down verbatim while he was learning his craft as a young reporter on the Dumfries Courier. This also was an innovation for the Glasgow press.

'Previously,' according to an admiring contemporary, 'reports of public meetings, no matter how important, and of public events, no matter how interesting, had been of the most meagre description, but on Pagan's coming to our city all this was altered. He gave extended reports of every matter of interest, and the public, unaccustomed to this kind of treatment were agreeably surprised and warmly appreciated his efforts.'

By this example he was later hoist with his own petard; for years later as Editor – with such a routh of writers at his command as Outram never dreamed of – he grew more parsimonious with his column inches, and preached constantly to his staff on the text, 'Brevity is the great thing.'

His other *tour de force* about this time was his full and immediate reporting of the General Assembly debates during the controversies of the Disruption, where again the problem, which he solved to the confusion of his colleagues, was to get his copy from Edinburgh to Glasgow in time for the next issue.

It was no doubt James Pagan's long preparation for his promotion, during which he became an authority on the history and moods of Glasgow, and identified himself anonymously but completely with the paper, that made him when he came to office perhaps the most significant Editor of these two hundred years. Great changes, technical and professional, were on their way; and he saw them coming. It is not possible, nor would it be discreet, to measure what editorial influence Pagan enjoyed over his editor, how much he encouraged, or even guided and even goaded Outram in his reluctance to contemplate change. He certainly was in effective control for the last five years. Suffice it to say (before proceeding to the excursions and agitations of his own editorship) that during the period from 1839 to 1856 what was graceful in the Glasgow Herald was Outram, and what was down-to-earth was Pagan.

James Pagan

So much for Pagan, the reporter: Pagan the Editor changed and enhanced the impact and the authority of the paper; he vastly increased its coverage of the news; he developed the leading article, and he indulged his readers with such antiquarian and historical reminiscence about Glasgow as is still one of its richest sources of local colour. He also turned the Glasgow Herald into a daily paper; a change, this, of such enduring importance that we take it a little out of its context, and advance a couple of years into his official editorship, to January 1859, and take a look at one of those minor civil wars which from time to time add interest, if not indeed a measure of excitement, to the newspaper trade.

Four years earlier Outram, Pagan and Morrison had reacted without excessive excitement to the withdrawal of the Stamp Duty. They just waited to see what would happen, and in the meantime reduced the price to 3d, and added Wednesday to the two established publication days of Monday and Friday. There were three other papers whose competition was of no consequence. These were the Bulletin, (Editor, George Troup), the Morning Journal (Editor, Robert Somers), and the Gazette, organ of the Free Kirk party (Editor, Peter Mackenzie, another voluminous Glasgow anecdotalist).

There was, however, a fourth, the North British Daily Mail, which had been a thorn in Pagan's professional side for the better part of ten years, and was now punishing the Herald, not only in circulation, but in being on time with the news. For example, in the case of Madeleine Smith, Pagan maintained that while his reports were infinitely superior, fuller, and more accurate, the Mail, being daily, and cheaper, had three times the Herald's circulation.

What followed is graphically and adequately illustrated in the cartoon which was bequeathed to me ten years ago, when James Pagan's grand-daughter-in-law sent it with the covering note: 'My late husband (Dr Mark Stewart) had the enclosed among his mother's papers. She evidently considered it worth preserving. She was the daughter of James Pagan (1811–1870) a former editor of the Glasgow Herald. I send the cartoon to you to place among old records, if it is of sufficient interest.'

The cartoon recording the local rivalries when the Glasgow Herald went on sale, daily, at one penny.

The decision to go daily was made in August 1858, and the necessary tooling-up took three or four months, during which time there were meetings with Gunn of the Mail, who expressed himself as content with Pagan's intention to publish at twopence (the same price as the Mail) from the beginning of January. In December the proposed changes in price, size and frequency were detailed in the paper and in a flood of circulars to newsagents and distributors – an innocent vanity that played straight into the hands of Robert Gunn, who was clearly before his time as a tactician in circulation games.

The new Herald was due on the streets on the morning of Monday, 3 January. Planning was complete, and much of the make-up was already on the 'stone' when on Friday, 31 December, the Mail announced that its issue on Monday would cost only a penny.

It was panic stations at 28 St Vincent Place, where the Herald, now on its move westwards, had just settled in, with the expectation of still more expansion. There was a round-up of shareholders who met on Saturday morning, and willy-nilly agreed that the price should also come down to a penny. The problem was how to let this be known in time to circumvent the competition. Placards were hastily run off and messengers were sent all over town to display them at all the churches on Sunday.

There was also a bit of urgent resetting in the caseroom, so that the 'lead' in bold italics would be:

Monday Morning, January 3

We this day publish the first number of the Glasgow Daily Herald, and we take this opportunity of intimating very respect-fully that circumstances have arisen which point out to us the expediency of reducing the price of the paper to

ONE PENNY

each number unstamped. The reduction begins with this Day. The 'Herald' of Monday and Friday will be printed on a sheet of eight pages as at present, and the 'Herald' of Tuesday, Wednes-day, Thursday and Saturday will be printed on a sheet of four pages, but whenever a pressure of news shall arise on these occasions the four-page sheet will be extended to meet the emergency. We have taken measures to provide machinery com-petent to meet the demand of a vastly extended circulation.

This was an expensive expediency, in the short term, for although circulation did increase, the penny price meant that the profits for 1859 went down by over 30 per cent. But that was soon put right.

James Pagan was *de facto* Editor from 1854. That means the Crimean War, and while it was no doubt the broadly cultured and wider-read gifts of Outram that produced the suitable allusions for the editorial comment on the enemy, it was the executive chief reporter who had to endure the frustration of wondering where the next news was coming from – and how late it would be.

One may question if it was Pagan who at the start of the crisis turned to Sir Austen Henry Layard, the Middle Eastern archaeologist, and the excavator of Nimrod's prehistoric mounds at Nineveh on the Tigris, for the nicely biased quotation that 'Turkey has done more in 50 years than Russia in 150 to promote civilisation.' What he was concerned with was the fact, as he complained in a leading article, that: 'One of our despatches from Balaclava may take a week or a couple of months before it reaches Constantinople, whereas the Russians, using Tartar couriers, whose speed is proverbial, get the news to Moscow in an incredibly short space of time, and hence it is telegraphed with the rapidity of lightning to St Petersburg and Berlin.'

It was from these Russian despatches that the Herald first heard of the charge of the Light Brigade, reported as a total defeat of our light cavalry. British despatches on the charge turned up nearly three weeks later, and the Herald had the keenest cause to envy its junior contemporary, The Times, that had William Howard Russell on the battlefield as war correspondent to point the blunders and detail the braveries, and to illuminate his eye-witness accounts with such enduring reporter's inspirations as 'the thin red line'. Not that the Herald went without its first-hand stories. It just had to wait a long time for them. These were the letters home which were the established stand-by of the provincial newspapers in the days before field censorship laid a curb upon the genre in the First World War. There were promising pens among the ranks in the Crimea, and James Pagan gave them their head. He may indeed have murmured 'Whaur's your Willie Russell noo?' when he subbed and sent one such letter to the printers. It was from a soldier of the 93rd Sutherland Highlanders, himself one of the thin red line at Balaclava, writing to his cousin in Glasgow, and telling him that 'Waterloo was not so hot as our storming of the heights above the Alma. We were tired out. If the enemy had marked properly the half of us would never have seen the top of the hill. We shouted and charged until we got within 200 yards of the enemy and then opened on them in a dreadful manner, and as hot as they gave us. They could not make out what we were. They took us for cavalry by our feathers and our bare legs and formed square . . . . Lord Raglan said we would never gain the heights.'

The Glasgow Herald had what might be described as a proprietary interest in the Indian Mutiny, since Pagan's predecessor had been the first cousin of Sir James Outram, the chief commissioner of Oudh, a renowned old India hand, and the generous general who temporarily deprived himself of his military command and served as a civil volunteer so that his subordinate comrade-in-arms, General Henry Havelock, might have the glory of leading the first relief of Lucknow.

The Herald stood staunch with the Raj, and James Pagan, now regularly editorialising, confessed to a measure of mystification. 'The

Generals Outram and Havelock greet Glasgow-born General Campbell at Lucknow, 17 November 1857.

Natives,' he wrote, 'had no natural ground of resentment against the British; they had no nepotism to oppose, and no emancipation to hope for. What has made them mutiny? – An ignorant disregard of their own welfare, and a wilful over-looking of all the peace, comforts and prosperity which they had experienced and were in prospect of from British rule.' Nor was he particularly enamoured of the subsequent restraint of the Governor-General Lord Canning (nicknamed 'Clemency Canning') whose more moderately expressed opinions on suitable retaliation upon the mutineers were denounced in his columns as 'weak, temporising, and full of false and sickly sentiment'.

Then, in 1860, the Herald engaged its first war correspondent. It was a tentative, adventitious contract. The sentiment for Italian self-government was running high in Scotland at that time, and nowhere more warmly than in the Glasgow Herald. There was a local angle – a trick that Pagan never missed – and he got in touch with a Rothesay man who, he heard, was going with a contingent of Scotch volunteers to lend Garibaldi a hand in the war of Italian Liberation. We do not know what the fee was; but the brief was simple, and somewhat unusual in a professional who was much given to advising his writers in matters of style and approach. 'I have no hints,' he wrote, 'to give you as to the manner of conducting your correspondence; but I would desire to have as much as possible reference to the Scottish companies.'

In the American Civil War, the next year, the Herald's sympathies to begin with were with the South, which was perhaps natural enough in view of the older associations with the tobacco and cotton trade. And Pagan was rather more blunt in his reply to an offer of despatches by a reporter/war-correspondent on the staff of the Scottish American Journal of New York. 'You judge rightly in saying that I am not disposed to pay more than a guinea a week for correspondence from America. I may remind you that you are already anticipated both by the Telegraph and the newspapers; the former, of course, you cannot attempt to cope with.'

By this time Pagan had an editorial assistant, James Hastie Stoddart (himself later to be Editor), who was of a more liberal cast of mind, and he guided his editor into such a reluctant neutrality as to persuade him to instruct his correspondents to 'write in as friendly and inoffensive tone as you can about the North'. On other matters – including Sabbath observance, on which he took a practical and permissive line – his instruction was: 'Our great object is to exhibit dignity, moderation and good sense.'

The trial of Madeleine Smith aroused intense public interest. The Herald published lengthy reports and commented in a less than detached way on the result.

chapter 7

CRIME AND (SOME) PUNISHMENT

WHILE JAMES PAGAN was in charge there occurred three of Glasgow's most cherished murderous *causes célèbres*. These were the trials of Madeleine Smith and of Jessie McLachlan, and the trial and execution of Dr Edward William Pritchard. So far as news values were concerned, Pagan's judgment was impeccable; and the Herald's near verbatim reports during the nine days of the trial of Madeleine in Edinburgh were much superior to those of his daily rivals. There are – and have indeed always been – those who feel that when it came to passing editorial opinion on matters criminous he was not free from bias or prejudice, particularly if the subject under scrutiny had the taint of being foreign. Nor for that matter was he totally impartial when the choice of blame lay between a member of the rising middle class and one of the lower working orders. Considerably more than a century later, it does not now pain us too much to admit that the Herald has one undoubted bloody murderer on its editorial conscience; and that it went out of its way to find explanations, if not indeed excuses, for the extremely hearty carnal appetite of another.

The case of Madeleine Smith, accused of murdering her lover – the lovely, lubricious details of which it is surely no longer necessary to rehearse – fell in the summer of 1857, and coincided with what must have been the beginning of the Editor's campaign to turn the leading article – which had until then consisted of the occasional brief and passing comment – into an impressive, challenging and if need be fearless, feature of his newspaper. At a slightly later stage in his incumbency when he had a talented assistant at his beck and call, it is not possible to identify surely the hand that wrote the anonymous leaders, but we know that he had the genius of delegation. As his obituary put it, 'He did a large and most important portion of the literary work of the paper by giving instructions as to how subjects should be treated, sometimes supplying forcible illustrations, sententious expressions and telling anecdotes, of which his store was inexhaustible.'

But in the year after the death of George Outram he was on his own; and therefore to him alone belongs the credit (if that be the correct word) for the editorial in the Glasgow Herald for 10 July 1857, drawing its lesson from the 'Not Proven' escape of Madeleine Smith, which can be quoted *in extenso* without apology, since it illustrates the more leisured approach and style of the times as well as confirming the particular biases which some have found in Pagan's views:

> This verdict, as all men know, may be interpreted as if the jury had said, 'We little question the prisoner's guilt but we desiderate that entirely complete and unmistakable legal proof of it which is necessary to satisfy our conscience in a matter of life and death.' This verdict, we have no doubt, will be satisfactory to all who have paid an enlightened attention to the evidence produced at the trial of this wretched girl. The awful tale of immorality and unrestrained appetite is concluded. The dreadful and disquieting record of wantonness and tergiversation is closed, but it will be long before the cloud of horror which her case flung over her native city will be dispersed. She is doomed to life-long repentance and may Heaven in its good time give her peace of mind.
>
> Madeleine Smith has passed out of the hands of justice, and her conscience is now her only tormentor. But does anyone believe that the story of her young life cannot be efficacious for good or evil? Will her deeds have no effect upon the thoughts and actions of the youth of her own and the future time?
>
> The tale which has been nine days telling in Edinburgh has left its impress upon the minds of thousands of persons, and it depends upon the care which all parents bestow upon their children whether the record may not work woe to many yet unborn. It is evident from the letters read in court that Madeleine Smith

Madeleine Smith, the tall figure fourth from the left, with her family.

had strong and ardent feelings of respect for her parents, but at the same time there seems to have been a deficiency on her part and to this cause must, beyond all doubt, be attributed the clandestine manner in which her intercourse with her seducer was carried on. We have no doubt that she knew the principles of religion which was by precept and example constant in the observance of its exterior duties; but is also evident that the 'weightier matters of the law' were little valued or practised, if understood, by her. She fell into the snare planted for her by a vain and boastful braggart, and we know not what arts may have been employed to lead her away from the paths of innocence. But that sad end was attained, and she fell; and all that followed was to avoid the anger of her parents and the chance of a public exposure of her incontinence. We have said we know not what arts may have been used by L'Angelier to attain his evil purpose, but he came to his death, and whether by suicide or not is now beyond human ken. Though his arts may never be known, it would be a vast importance to ascertain, if it were possible, how much he had acquired of the vile knowledge to effect seduction which is so extensively diffused and put into practice in France. This is no place to enter into details regarding the hideous pollution which is so rife in France and which has so largely eaten into the moral and social life of Frenchmen. L'Angelier was of French extraction, if not French by birth, and his mind received its first ideas and manners in Jersey which is almost a French colony. It is not far removed from the Gallic shores and it has such a constant intercourse with the coast of France, and is so full of French

L'Angelier and Madeleine as contemporary cartoonists saw them.

people that it would not be hard to believe that much of the abominable wisdom which pertains to the people of the Continent may have penetrated, along with *proscits* and political refugees, into the island. We do not moot these matters for the purpose of palliating the career of Madeleine Smith, but rather, if possible, for arriving at some solution of the awful facts which have been revealed and indicated in the course of the most laborious investigation which has just terminated.

The French people are notoriously addicted to the use of cosmetics and persons who knew the deceased, L'Angelier, say that he looked as though he had been in the habit of using something for his complexion. Did he initiate the Scottish girl into the mysteries of arsenic as an improver of the skin? She said she used arsenic for her complexion. Was this a lie coined for the purpose of excuse, as vile as those lying letters in which she one day professed the most ardent love for L'Angelier, while she was encouraging the addresses and owning an affection for another? Was her knowledge of arsenic as a cosmetic solely derived from Professor Johnston's writings? It is now too late for the ends of justice to inquire into these matters, but it is not too late for public safety. The crime Madeleine Smith was tried for is unparalleled in the annals of modern legal practice, and, moreover, there were many circumstances brought to light which gave the whole proceedings of the girl and her lover an unBritish character. Supposing that she poisoned L'Angelier, can anything be conceived more terribly evil than that after her terror lest her clandestine intercourse should be revealed to her parents and to her other affianced husband she should assume the manners and language of love while preparing the means of ending his life?

The deep cunning of such a deed is so utterly devoid of parallel that it shocks the moral sense and reads more like a page of mediaeval history of Italy than a story of Scottish life in the nineteenth century. We are pleased that this awful charge is not proven. Would to God it be not true.

The whole circumstances of the trial, its momentous importance, its extraordinary duration, the profound anxiety evinced throughout the nation to follow the proceedings of the court from day to day, are all alike remarkable and not less so in the astonishing circumstance that *ladies* sat in the court during every day while the vile and obscene story was unravelled by judges, advocates and lawyers.

Preachers, teachers and educational reformers ought to think of all these things. It is not alone a question of life or death to one weak young woman that is concerned. The moral weal or woe of thousands must and will be affected by the life of this girl and by the terrible revelations of the trial. Just as a stone thrown into a lake agitates the water until the ripple breaks on every one of its shores, so will the story of L'Angelier's vile life and death, and the wanton if not more wicked evil in that of Madeleine Smith, agitate for good or evil the moral ocean of human life.

We had intended to say a few words relative to the manner in which the prosecution and the defence were conducted by the Lord Advocate and the Dean of Faculty, but our limits forbid and besides the subject is too large to be treated properly at the end of an article; suffice it, therefore, that we express our high admiration of the admirable speech delivered for the defence by the learned advocate last referred to, and we think it will remain a masterpiece of Scottish forensic eloquence.

This was no doubt exactly how the West End of Glasgow at least thought it felt about a scandal that had come much too close to home. There was not, however, the same unanimity some four years later in the aftermath of the Sandyford Murder when Jessie McLachlan was convicted of the slaughter of Jessie Macpherson, the servant girl in the residence of an up-and-coming commercial family, a few steps west of Charing Cross (where Madeleine had bought her arsenic in the shop of Currie the Chemist).

We need not any longer doubt that the hand that swung the axe was that of the lewd and aged father of the family, James Fleming, who had been left alone with the girl while the others went on holiday to the Coast. During a boozy carouse in the basement, and while Jessie McLachlan, a visiting friend of the servant, was out looking for more drink, the first assault took place, and the murder was completed during another of her brief absences. Jessie McLachlan was identified and involved by reason of some pawned silver and her possession of one of the dead girl's dresses.

James Fleming, who became the prime Crown witness, was first arrested but was released after eight days, and Jessie tholed her assize alone, to the indignation of much of the public and all the newspapers save the Glasgow Herald. The Herald persisted throughout the trial, which it reported verbatim, keeping up to date with hourly editions, in referring to Fleming as 'the old innocent'.

'The newspapers,' it is recorded, 'had each other by the throat.' When Jessie was convicted and condemned the Herald supported the judge's sentence, against the opinion of the North British Daily Mail and the Morning Journal, which were of the opinion that Fleming had been art and part of the crime, with the result that 'the Glasgow Herald office was frequently in danger'.

In the meantime Auld Fleming had been spirited away to the family holiday house at Rothesay, where, it is said, he used to lurk by the garden hedge to accost the commuters homeward bound off the Clyde paddlers, and ask them: 'Have they no' hangit that wumman yet?'

His popularity, indeed, was similar to the Herald's own, when it praised a Commission that upheld the verdict and sentence – and the

Jessie McLachlan, from a portrait published after the trial.

James Fleming, from a drawing made in Court.

crowd made bonfires of the paper in the street outside the office in St Vincent Place. The death sentence was eventually commuted to life imprisonment.

Edward William Pritchard, a surgeon of low professional repute and a seducer of servant girls, practised in Sauchiehall Street in a house bought for him by his wife's mother. He poisoned both his mother-in-law and his wife with aconite, and himself wrote their death certificates, in which he specified 'apoplexy' and 'gastric fever'.

When Dr Pritchard in 1865 'faced the Monument', as they used to say when a felon was topped in Jail Square opposite the Nelson Memorial, the Herald concentrated on in-depth reporting rather than on moralising. From the moment of the arrest of 'the human crocodile', who shed tears over the corpses of his victims, it seems to have been *au fait* with his every move and mood. Thus: 'On being arrested and consigned to gaol his main regret was that he could not be favoured with a supply of pomatum for the trimming of his beard and hair.' And, when first arrested in Glasgow, 'previous to retiring to rest, and before the room was vacated by the officers, the Doctor engaged in prayer'.

The Herald covered his execution handsomely in two-and-a-half columns of detailed and moderately macabre descriptive reporting.

Old buildings in the High Street, Glasgow – 1868

chapter 8

PROPERTIES AND THE ELECTRIC TELEGRAPH

ONE WAY or another technology was waxing moderately rampant in the 1850's and 60's, imposing its own expansive demands upon such newspapers as the Glasgow Herald, which has always properly prided itself on keeping pace with the times. Sometimes it even managed to be that little ahead, as in the matter of the electric telegraph.

This, indirectly, involved James Pagan and his partners for the first time in property transactions, which started with the flitting in 1858 from the cosy purlieus of Spreull's Court. The feeling had been growing that the Herald owed it to itself to be moving westwards along with its commercial and mercantile peers. And it was Adam Morrison, the wakeful sleeping partner, who did something about it. Until then all the premises occupied by the paper had been rented. Morrison put substance to the day-dreams by calling a meeting, early in the year, when he announced that he had in his own name bought a suitably extensive property at 28 St Vincent Place for £7400, and that he was ready to sell it at the same price to the company. The deal was clinched, another couple of thousand pounds was spent on alterations to accommodate the larger machinery that a daily paper with a mounting circulation would require. They raised a loan of £5000 from the City of Glasgow Assurance Company, and the speculation so justified itself that within four years the paper had wiped out the debt from its profits.

One of the conveniences of St Vincent Place was its handiness to Royal Exchange Square, whence the Intelligence Department of the Electric and International Company and the Magnetic Telegraph Company distributed its press telegrams by messenger at half the ordinary rate. These companies, along with the United Kingdom Telegraph Company ran their own news collecting service in London, of which the Herald took advantage to the tune of 4000 words a day; mainly a parliamentary summary, and general, commercial, sporting and social news.

As a back-up to this shared source Pagan in 1861 sent his own editorial man to London. This was William Brown, who was in effect the forerunner to the establishment of the London Office – an ambition which the Editor nourished for a decade, prepared for, and arranged, but he died just too soon, and like Moses was allowed to see but not to enter into his promised land. This London presence was so productive that, just about the time in the mid-sixties that the Government took over the telegraphs (and the Press Association was formed by the provincial newspapers to take over the Telegraph Intelligence Service) the Herald leased a special wire from the Magnetic Company, which became operational on 14 March 1866. The immediate result, according to the report on the rest of that year's trading was 'a large numerical increase in circulation'.

When the next move was made into Buchanan Street in 1868 – where the paper was to remain for the next 112 years – it enjoyed another minor triumph in one-upmanship; for the special wire (which was now rented from the Post Office at £500 a year) was installed in the new offices. We have the authority of the Postmaster-General's official report for 1869 that the Glasgow Herald's was one of the only two offices in the United Kingdom whose wires were carried into their own premises 'thereby dispensing with the service of messengers'. It should be added that the other pioneer thus complimented was the Scotsman.

In 1867, with the circulation climbing beyond 25,000, with the offices overcrowding, St Vincent Place had become inadequate, so the partners sold it at a profit of more than £2000, and bought a site at 65 Buchanan Street, for £23,000. Since the Herald stayed there so long, it deserves a little more than the mere note of a postal address.

The area, some 15,000 square feet, stretched all the way through from Buchanan Street to Mitchell Street, and had already made its contribution to folk-lore. The owner was M.M. Pattison, one of the

Two aspects of Victorian Glasgow – a lane off High Street in 1868; the interior of a professor's drawing room at No. 7 The University.

more enterprising of the early Buchanan Street entrepreneurs, who in 1830 had the idea of running a market there. A covered entry led through the building on the frontage into an open square, where he built an arcade with small shops on its four sides; and in the middle a great stone fresh-water tank from which he sold live fish. When this piazza lost its novelty he rebuilt the square, covering it with the Monteith Rooms, a first storey suite of assembly and exhibition halls, approached by a flight of wide stairs leading down into Buchanan Street.

Under the new ownership the site behind the Buchanan Street facade was cleared right back to Mitchell Street. The building that was raised there has lasted ever since, but not without some considerable alterations, both internal and external, most notably at the hands of Charles Rennie Mackintosh, who will be considered a generation or so later – though at some peril since he is at present riding the crest of a cult-wave.

The peculiarity of the Herald, until recently, was that though its front door seemed to lead into the Victorian mahogany halls of Buchanan Street, this was an illusion – and always had been. It was explained by Mr Pattison, the former owner, who attended the festival dinner at which the nearly-completed new buildings were celebrated. Proposing the toast of Mr Baird, the architect, he said: 'The new premises possess somewhat the misfortune of the person who, according to Charles Lamb, had his forehead at the back of his head; for their chief front, and their only one so far as Mr Baird's labours are concerned, is at the back in Mitchell Street instead of where it naturally should be, in Buchanan Street.'

Pagan, who did not live long enough fully to enjoy the splendours of his new domain, was well satisfied, and added: 'You are by this time so well acquainted with these stately halls, that I need say little more than that they are not rivalled by any printing house in the kingdom.'

In anticipation of Buchanan Street, two Hoe eight-feeder printing presses were ordered at £9000, with a discount of £2750 on the old machines; and on 9 November 1868, the Glasgow Herald came out of the new premises, printed on the new machines. It also reached the newsagents with contents bills for display. This was a gimmick which Pagan adopted with great reluctance and a distrust of the buying public (or a proportion thereof) who, he suspected, might be content with the 'capsulated' news of the poster. Indeed, he objected so strongly that he tried to dissuade the Scotsman and the Manchester Guardian, and relented only when they reported increased sales.

Except in one respect all Pagan's newspaper innovations were a success, or the foundation for future fortune. But he did slip up once. That was in 1865 when the North British Daily Mail, which had some years before outflanked him in the matter of the penny-daily, published an evening paper. The presumption admitted but one response, which came on 29 April 1865, with the Glasgow Evening Herald, and

The Herald's frontage in
Buchanan Street. The famous
Rennie Mackintosh tower and frontage
is to the rear in Mitchell Street.

this announcement: 'Till three days ago nothing was further from our
thoughts than entering on the field recently taken up and cultivated
by our young contemporary, the Evening Citizen; but now that one of
the established morning papers has commenced the issue of an evening sheet at the lowest possible price, we feel that the situation has
materially changed, and we owe it to ourselves to meet this new paper
by a similar publication. Although we have been thus dragged, as it
were, into the issue of the Evening Herald, we shall spare no exertion
to render that paper worthy of the favour and confidence of the public.'

They were bonny fechters then, jealous and quick in quarrel, all
credit to them, but in this engagement there were no winners, only two
losers. On the same day, Saturday, 13 November, just seven and a bit
months later, the Herald and Mail both cried quits and stopped printing their evening papers.

While on the subject of near misses, there is one other undertaking
which James Pagan started, but failed to pursue to the irretrievable
loss of the Glasgow Herald. It will be remembered that when John

Mennons cut his ties with the Advertiser he took the bound files with him; and when he died his family regarded them as its personal property, and they vanished. One result of this was that for more than a hundred years, the Herald did not even know the date of its first issue; and was in fact so wrong in its calculation that the centenary was celebrated (and that lavishly, with a great public banquet in St Andrew's Hall), a whole year too soon on 27 January 1882.

A grandson of John Mennons remembered having seen the files at Greenock where his father at the time had run a local newspaper. This Mark Antony Francis Mennons was a patent agent in Paris, and while on a visit to Glasgow in 1868, he visited James Pagan, and agreed to the suggestion that the proper place for the files would be the new offices in Buchanan Street. Unfortunately, there the matter rested – for fourteen years.

Mark Mennons, indeed, seems to have gone back to Paris thinking that the bargain was in train. His own interest in his grandfather's paper thus revived, he took one of the earliest files with him. Then in 1882 Mark Mennons, still in Paris, was invited to the centenary celebrations; and in the course of correspondence with the Manager, Alexander Sinclair, he expressed surprise that the paper was still without its files. To this day nobody knows what became of them. But what about the volume (perhaps the very first) which he had taken back as a memento to Paris? Unfortunately during the siege of Paris in 1870 the Germans burnt down his house on the outskirts of the city, with the loss of everything that had been in it.

The siege of Paris was not all frustration for the paper, however, for the Herald was able to regale its readers with special eye-witness reports from within the city. We do not now know who exactly the correspondent was; only that he got his despatches out by balloon by drifting them over the Prussian lines.

It was as much in the role of encourager of talent as in that of a writer himself – though he did that too – that James Pagan left his mark on the paper. He was a natural historian and antiquarian and sought to capture in the columns of the paper a recollection that was in danger of slipping irretrievably away. To that end, he delved into the proceedings of the Dean of Guild Court, from which, in a long series of articles, there emerged a comprehensive picture not only of the physical growth of Glasgow, but of the men and institutions that were at its making. These, with reminiscences and historical sketches, he edited and compiled to become the three invaluable volumes of 'Glasgow Past and Present'. Along with this work Pagan made a couple of substantial contributions to the Glasgow bookshelf. In his early days on the Herald, he was asked to provide captions to a collection of lithograph views of the town. These notes, however, so expanded themselves that the original intention of a limited publication was dropped, and the prints, instead, became the illustrations for his comprehensive 'Sketches of the History of Glasgow', a work, we are told, much

While this is not an exclusive portrait of 'our man in Paris', it is an approximately contemporary illustration of how he got his despatches out during the Prussian siege of 1870.

appreciated by Queen Victoria, who kept and perused her 'superbly bound' presentation copy on the royal yacht. His guide to Glasgow Cathedral, commissioned at the time of the restoration of the building in 1849, remained for long the definitive handbook.

He also commissioned the splendidly regular correspondence of two long-memoried literate old men. Of these the more venerable was Robert Reid, who wrote under the pen-name of 'Senex'. He, whom we have already quoted, had a vivid personal memory of the day the first copies of the Glasgow Advertiser were distributed by John Mennons himself in the Tontine Coffee House, and along the plainstanes round the Cross. 'Senex' died in 1865 at the age of 92, and could boast that in his childhood, he 'sat upon the knees of ancient men and women who rejoiced that they were the last of the true Scots, for they had lived at a time when Scotland was an independent kingdom, and when her Parliament met in Edinburgh'. And he had a well-storied remembrance of men 'still hale and robust' who had been out in the '45; not to mention the Tobacco Barons and the nearly-first-hand tales of the French Revolution and the Reign of Terror.

Robert Reid – 'Senex', who remembered the first appearance of the Glasgow Advertiser in the streets, and whom James Pagan promoted as the great Glasgow reminiscencer.

He wrote, also out of the treasure-trove of a family history of four hundred years of Glasgow burgesses, Deacons, Bailies and Lords Provost. And his own varied business career in the town began with an apprenticeship in the muslin-making trade under David Dale. These antiquities were incorporated into the third volume of 'Glasgow Past and Present', along with those of James Pagan's other senior contributor 'Aliquis'. He – also of old Glasgow stock, and a nephew of Benjamin Mathie, John Mennons' first partner and legal adviser – was Dr Mathie Hamilton, whose hobby was Glasgow memorabilia, and whose profession had been medicine which he practised in South America, where he was head of the medical staff of the Peruvian Army.

Pagan's own writing, of which indeed there was plenty, was competent rather than inspired. He left the purple passages to others; first to his dilettante editor Outram and latterly to his own assistant Stoddart. He concentrated upon what he himself cherished as 'solid common sense'. At the end of the day his warmest admirer and colleague wrote that while his 'literary efforts were always forcible and nervous, his gifts were not specially literary – though he had a quick ear for the ring of the true metal, and as quick a faculty in detecting the merely meretricious and base'.

As already mentioned, he preferred giving advice as to how subjects should be treated. And by all accounts these were plain enough. For example, it was perhaps natural in the Editor of a newspaper which came on the streets early on Monday morning (or even last thing on Sunday night) that he did not see eye to eye with the 'ultra-Sabbatarians'. His liberal attitude on this matter was described in some contemporary pulpits as 'Unitarian, Pantheist and Infidel'. He was 'the patron of irreligion and Sabbath profanation'. And in the same quarters, he was less than popular for his policy of giving a fair share in his columns to local Roman Catholic news and announcements.

This dispute came to a head in the mid-60's, about the time when Pagan had embarked on his brief experiment with the Glasgow Evening Herald. And the confrontation gave the Herald a historical Outram martyr, and what it has always claimed as a moral victory. The catalyst was James Robertson, a compositor, known as the 'Flea', who was a member of the Free Gorbals Church.

The Flea came into collision with the Fourth Commandment when, from holding a week-day job, he was transferred to the Glasgow Herald, which involved his working at the case on Sundays. It was a move that did not disturb his own conscience. Indeed, he hardly thought it worth mentioning; and the transgression was not discovered until the minister, having noticed his regular absence from the evening service, learned from his wife that he was at his work in St Vincent Place.

James Pagan always believed in full reporting. In the days that followed James Robertson got nine nearly verbatim columns in his own paper; with for good measure such a leading article as must have warmed the censorious ears of the fathers and brethren.

The Kirk Session excluded him from the privileges and sacraments of the Church. He appealed to the Synod, which confirmed the excommunication. So he took his case to the General Assembly, where, not unaided, he pleaded his own case. At the bar of the Assembly, the voice may have been the voice of the Flea; but the hand as it appeared in the brief from which he made his submissions was Pagan's. The arguments, the facts, and the interpretations were set out plainly; and so unanswerably that the Moderator was moved more than once to rebuke some of the reverend delegates for applauding.

The Flea's first point was that the Glasgow Herald fitted perfectly into the category of a work of necessity and mercy. He went on to mention other labourers who enjoyed the same exemptions: 'Harnessing of horses and driving of carriages on Sunday is as much a matter of secular enjoyment as occupation in the manual preparation of a journal for the press. . . . My own minister himself hired a carriage and drove to Paisley on a communion Sabbath. Moderator, why should that be wrong in me which those who are my judges do themselves or permit others to do? . . . Which is the more necessary, the publication of a newspaper, the suppression of which would paralyse the whole social, political and mercantile arrangements of the community . . . or the cooking of hot dinners, or the performance of all the drudgery of a week-day work in a private home?'

This was too much for the Moderator, Dr Robert Smith Candlish, a giant of the Disruption, who was not accustomed to contradiction. 'I object,' he replied, 'to being catechised as regards my consistency, or the consistency of other members of the Church.' He put his motion and the Flea remained excommunicated.

The Herald did not take this judgment meekly. It was probably Stoddart, the assistant editor, duly primed by Pagan, who wrote the leading article which said, along with other unpalatable truths: 'Men like James Robertson have a higher tribunal to appeal to than any ecclesiastical court – a tribunal that will settle according to their real merits all questions of Sunday work – and not only for him and his class, but for the Church itself.'

Both in and out of the office Pagan seems to have been a good companion. He was shrewd and he was genial, and he kept some of the tedium out of editorial conferences by telling apt stories, citing forcible illustrations, and then adding, if on reflection he found them a bit strong – 'But don't put that in.' He was a snuff taker, much attached to a silver snuff-box which he had received many years earlier from the printers of Dumfries when he left to make a brief foray into a printing business in London. The snuff-box served a double purpose, for it contained not only the 'best brown Taddy', but small bits of paper covered with shorthand notes, 'constantly reminding him, when he opened it, of some little business to see about'. He did not socialise much, nor take great pleasure in public appearances; though he did, in agreeable company, sing songs, including in his repertoire some of George Outram's comic lyrics which had been set to music.

James Pagan was not robust, and indeed had been ailing for five or six years when, after a short, acute illness, he died in February 1870.

chapter 9

THE ACADEMIC INTERLUDE

CHANGES FOLLOWED the death of Pagan, including an error of judgment which, fortunately, it was possible to correct before the consequences became too disastrous for a concern which was, perhaps, growing a little too rapidly for comfort. The error was the appointment of William Jack, and the next five years (reckoned in strictly commercial terms) were not too good for the paper. At first glance, one is tempted to blame him, but his shade is entitled to claim a generous plea in mitigation. One must, indeed, go so far as to say that he was as disappointed in his employers as they were in him.

Editorially, he seems to have been above reproach; but the passing of Pagan also heralded the end of the long, mildly autocratic era of the 'actor-manager', and the emergence of a wider management structure. Such authoritative assessments of Jack's editorship as have come down to us are front-office opinions based on the returns of revenue and circulation, which in truth were discouraging enough. These historians were two managers, who between them served the paper for more than a hundred years. The first of these was Alexander Sinclair (a person of great importance and influence in our chronicle) who, without mentioning a name, but in an unmistakable context wrote: 'It has many a time been the misfortune of those concerned in a newspaper enterprise to discover too late that experience in the work – a long apprenticeship – is essential to the making of a capable newspaper editor; the assumption of the editorial chair by an inexperienced man has repeatedly turned out a failure, and a danger to the property he controlled.'

The obvious successor, to whom that criticism could not have been applied, was James Hastie Stoddart, who had been Pagan's right hand man for eight years, and who had already put his own literary and political mark on the Herald. But the partners, most of them the trustees of former editors and shareholders – and all but three of these absentees – were eager for a change from the old order in which all policy was dictated by the editor/proprietor, his only obligation to provide his sleeping partners with periodic accounts of costs, profits, circulation figures and advertising revenue.

Two executives were appointed: Robert Gourlay to represent the Pagan Trust, and the above mentioned Alexander Sinclair, who was then the counting-house manager. Having passed over Stoddart, they, with Adam Morrison, one of the sons of George Outram's old legal adviser, set out to find an editor who would fit their specification; namely a person of consequence, literary talent, sound political principles and hopefully, some business acumen.

After a short search, they agreed that they had found their man in William Jack, Professor of Natural Philosophy in Owen's College, Manchester. Jack was a graduate of Glasgow University, a Fellow of Peterhouse, and a former inspector of schools. Three months after the death of Pagan, he was appointed Editor of the Herald, at a salary of £800 a year, and with the promise of a commission on the profits. He inherited a booming circulation of over 27,000, which had risen by 23,000 from the time Pagan took office, and an annual profit of £19,700, which had swollen from £7100 in the same time. He was engaged on a five-year contract, and joined with the expectation of becoming a partner. Indeed, he made his application for that privilege within two months of his appointment, and was turned down as hasty and presumptuous, a situation which did not improve his relationship with his employers.

He applied again in 1873, but with no better success. By that time, in fact, he had become the scapegoat for dissensions among the partners. His management came under extreme criticism. The circulation increased only by 500 copies a day; and although advertising improved, the annual profit fell by something of the order of £12,000.

It was more than a little hard that the responsibility for this was wished on him, because during this time the paper was saddled with vast and expensive expansions. The London office, of which Pagan had

William Jack

79

dreamed, had come into being at 97 Fleet Street. It had a staff which, starting modestly enough with James Walker, the paper's first London Editor (an office he held with distinction for 22 years), so increased with attention to Parliamentary and general reporting that, within three years, the Herald moved to 'more commodious premises' at 107 Fleet Street. By this time, the Herald had a front 'box' in the Press Galleries of both Houses. And since the coverage included the Law Lords there was the expense not only of enlarging the Parliamentary staff, but also of installing a second special direct wire into Buchanan Street. The London reporting now also included theatre and exhibition reviews, the paper's own coverage of State occasions; and 'a Lady correspondent'. To anticipate, but to indicate the trend and status of the London Office under Walker, the next Editor but one, Charles G. Russell, was able fairly to claim that the Glasgow Herald's London Letter was the best in the country.

Then, again during Jack's time, there were the costly preliminaries to a radical change in the printing machinery. This indeed was a negotiation, largely promoted by Alexander Sinclair, which with many interruptions and attacks of cold feet started at the beginning of 1871 and continued for seven years.

Editorially and politically this was not an exciting half-decade. The Herald had a composed inclination towards Gladstone rather than Disraeli, and indeed it was restraint rather than partial commitment in the matter of Kirk Disestablishment – a question whose emotional subtleties are now hard to recapture – that inspired the launching of a new conservative newspaper by a group of dedicated Glasgow Churchmen. This was the Glasgow News, at 67 Hope Street, which is of relevance to this story only because, though it failed as a morning paper, it became the Glasgow Evening News, which in turn led to the starting of the Evening Times. But that is a story that belongs to 1875 and to James H. Stoddart.

A disillusioned William Jack handed in his resignation in 1875 and left Buchanan Street to fill the more comfortable Chair of Mathematics at Glasgow University. For the record of his apparent unsuccess, we are indebted to the hard facts of Alexander Sinclair and of Alex McL. Ewing, who joined the counting house as a lad in 1884, and who was Managing Director when the 150th anniversary was celebrated in 1933.

There is, however, a more flattering contemporary professional opinion which got into print quite unobtrusively in 1909 when he moved from Glasgow University into 'cultured retirement'. 'As the Editor of the Herald he is due the credit of raising the tone of the paper, and giving it a position infinitely higher than that of a merely local journal. Without practical newspaper experience, he brought to the work of Editor a clear head, fertility of resource, and an amount of enterprise which would have been looked upon by his predecessor as suicidal recklessness. Added to these qualities, he had a ready pen and a suave and agreeable manner. During his short term of five years, the paper assumed a position which it had never before occupied, to hold its own as one of the first non-metropolitan journals in the country.'

The view all depends on where you happen to be standing.

Ewart Gladstone, whom J.H. Stoddart, devout Liberal though he was, put firmly in his political place. Gladstone is depicted here during his famous Midlothian Campaign of 1874.

chapter 10

THE CENTENARY

James Stoddart

IN THE PAST not much more has been recorded of James Hastie Stoddart, other than that he was a poet of sorts. He was more than that. He was a creative editor of independent mind; and unlike his predecessors was the editorial guru not of one, but of three newspapers, the Herald, the Weekly Herald and the Evening Times. And, not least so far as prestige was concerned, he presided over the vastly magisterial civic celebration of the centenary of the paper – albeit a year too soon.

He was a Liberal of such national respect that he was elected to the Reform Club 'without the ordeal of a ballot, at the instance of the Political Committee'. But, if Gladstone was wont to lecture Queen Victoria, Stoddart, when occasion demanded, was not blate to instruct Gladstone, and if necessary to put him bluntly in his place. When the Grand Old Man came to the Midlothian campaign in 1874, full of denunciation of the Turks and of the Government's Afghan policy, the Herald advised him, quite mildly, 'not to make too much of the Eastern question'.

Nor was the Herald particularly sold on his Little Englandism, and chose to be a mite sterner in denying that the burden of Empire was becoming too heavy to bear: 'The country is not conscious of the terrible exhaustion which the Right Honourable Gentleman declares it is experiencing, and will be apt to resent the imputation.' And the disillusion, drifting towards Liberal-Unionism, boiled over on the question of Irish Home Rule, when leading articles were moved in sorrow to disinherit him, saying: 'Who would have thought that the great leader of the Liberal Party would have agreed to buy off the treason of Irish-Americans and the agitation of the Parnellites by a sudden and what – considering all the circumstances – we are bound to call a base surrender?'

The final break, however, did not come until after Stoddart's day; and his displeasure with Gladstone was more kindly expressed than was his envoi to Disraeli, when he died in 1881: 'Certain points of his career cannot be defended on the ordinary perceptions of honour and truth.'

In most matters, including politics, the opinion of the Glasgow Herald under Stoddart was judicial, and indeed sometimes too balanced for the taste of more partisan readers, not least those most immovably thirled to the shibboleths of the native Church. Here, and particularly on the question of disestablishment, his impartiality, amounting some said to indifference, may have owed something to a recollection of the crow that he had once so effectively picked with the Free Kirk's General Assembly itself, in defence of the Outram Martyr, the Flea.

J.H. Stoddart, who was born in 1832, came from Sanquhar, where his parents 'belonged to the best class of the Scottish peasantry'. He was roundly educated, with a smattering of Latin and Greek, in the local school; and according to himself, he inherited his poetic bent from his mother who 'had an extensive acquaintanceship with the ballad literature of Scotland'.

Though he no doubt had his eye on it as his target from his childhood, his progress to the daily journalism, upon which he eventually laid a more sophisticated mark, was cautious and diligent. He left home as a lad for Edinburgh where he got a job as office boy in the counting house of the Scotsman. This initial, but brief, newspaper connection lasted only until he found himself a similar post with a chemical firm in Leith. Soon, however, he was back in Edinburgh, working with Messrs Bryden, the bellhangers, and showing such promise in this specialised and tintinnabulous trade, that, at the age of eighteen in 1850, he was sent to Glasgow to establish a West of Scotland branch of the business. He stayed with Bryden's twelve years, but in the meantime devoted his leisure to 'a course of self-education and of reading which might be said to range over the whole field of English literature and thought, speculative and otherwise'.

Then the dormant leader-writer stirred, and, having had some

General Ulysses S. Grant, who, regrettably without saying anything significant, inaugurated the new Hoe printing presses in Buchanan Street; but for sentimentalists it kept up the Herald's link with the U.S.A.

modest contributions accepted by the North British Daily Mail, he ventured more boldly into opinion and was accepted as an occasional editorial writer for the Scottish Banner, a short-lived journal promoting social improvement. With his toe thus in the door, he got to know James Geddes (one of Pagan's men who went on to flourish on the London Standard) and with his help became a Herald freelance. Four years later, at the age of thirty – and presumably when Geddes left for London – Stoddart was taken on to the staff at St Vincent Street as sub-editor. From then on it was plain sailing and plenty of writing for eight years until the Professor Jack interregnum, an aberration which Pagan's right hand man bore loyally and without any recorded complaint.

William Jack having taken his superficially regretted leave in the spring of 1875, Stoddart came into his own, and, along with Alexander Sinclair assumed the joint management of an operation in which they intended to brook no opposition. The immediate threat was the North British Daily Mail, which was turning out a too healthy circulation on its new rotary presses. And so their first retaliation was to reactivate the negotiations that had dawdled and died since 1871; and to place a firm order with Hoe of America for two rotary presses at £3300 each, capable of printing, cutting and folding 12,000 copies an hour; these to be delivered and in operation within a twelvemonth.

That settled, they then turned their attention to another threat. For ten years, and particularly after Pagan's unsuccessful venture in the field, the local tribunes of Outram had paraded a condescending tolerance for the Evening Citizen, 'our young contemporary'. But now the Evening News had come on the scene and looked like cornering a new and untapped market of Glasgow readers. The Evening Times was an instant, and satisfactorily embarrassing, success. It sold at a halfpenny and had an immediate circulation of more than 50,000. It was jocose and newsy, its editorial policy supervised from a benignly paternal distance by Stoddart, leaving its first Editor, William Freeland, a writer of thrillers and ballads in his spare time, a free hand in his choice of subjects, notably sport, 'to be criticised frankly on the grounds of principle alone'. Such subjects included striped stockings for women, and an irreverent analysis of the reformist theories of a strident teetotal minister from Greenock.

The immediate result of the runaway success of the Evening Times was such a demand upon the printing presses that a third, and much improved press was ordered. This urgent order was placed with Robert Hoe Junior himself, who was on a visit to this country, and was able to take personal note of special requirements, which included a capacity to print two different sizes of paper in succession – the four page Times and the eight page Herald.

The press was installed to schedule in 1877, and was about to be set going when Ulysses S. Grant, having retired from his fairly corrupt eight years' Presidency of the United States, stopped off during a world

tour to receive the freedom of the City of Glasgow. And, since the Hoes were American, Alexander Sinclair had the idea that it would be a nice compliment, as well as a useful bit of oneupmanship, to invite him to start the new machine. After a civic ceremony, he came across to Buchanan Street from the City Chambers, along with Mrs Grant and the Lord Provost, and duly pulled the lever. We would have liked to record a suitably impressive, presidential, obiter dictum, but all that U.S. Grant was heard to say was: 'I guess I have seen some such printing presses in New York.'

The Glasgow Herald staff reacted with more imagination, and during the succeeding years, until it was sold to a printer in Wales (where for all we know, it may still be doing its duty), that press was known as 'The General'.

The major sensation of the Stoddart regime, however, was the failure of the City of Glasgow Bank in 1878, a disaster which touched the Outram shareholders intimately but had the side-effect of providing their papers with a conspicuous scoop. The loss was of the order of £6,000,000, and, since the Bank was an unlimited company, the whole liability fell upon the 1200 shareholders, a majority of whom were the smaller business people of the town.

On the discovery in the early forenoon of 2 October that the bank had closed its door, the sensation was immediate, with Buchanan Street the concentration point for vociferous and anxious crowds demanding information. The Herald was in a position to give it. There was a full list of the shareholders in the paper's counting house, but whether it should be published was a heavy decision and one not to be made on the spot. But it was an urgent one, and so, while the list was being put into type, a sub-editor was sent in a hansom-cab to carry the news, and the responsibility, to the Editor-in-chief at his home. Stoddart said: 'Publish.' The Evening Times was on the streets by one o'clock, and that day's sales were more than 100,000 copies.

The failure of the City of Glasgow Bank in 1878 brought ruin to hundreds of investors. Two of the directors, Robert Stronach (left), manager, and Lewis Potter (right) each received 18 months imprisonment for falsifying the accounts. Five other directors were jailed for eight months.

85

There was, however, a less gratifying sequel when the liquidators got to work, and it transpired that one of the trustee shareholders of the Outram company held £3500 of City of Glasgow Bank stock. The sales and transfers which followed led to a revaluation of the company shares, a complex and protracted settlement which brought Alexander Sinclair and J.H. Stoddart into the partnership, with one £8000 share each. Further financial transactions (which may more conveniently be relegated to Appendix 2 from the well versed hand of the late A. McL. Ewing) indicate the growing prosperity of the concern most succinctly in the sale, soon after this, of one Outram share to James Kennedy of Doonholm (the home, in our day, of the famous herd of Aberdeen-Angus cattle) for £11,000.

It is, however, with the editorial Stoddart that we are most concerned, and perhaps his most significant achievement was the advancement of the political consequence of the Glasgow Herald. This came largely from his development of the London Letter, which ran regularly to four or five columns, dominated by Parliamentary news and comment, leavened with discreet fragments of fashionable gossip. Indeed the standing of the paper was such that when it came to the centenary celebration the public Parliamentary tribute bore that: 'The Glasgow Herald is amongst the very best of the penny provincial papers; and that means it is better than the London Press . . . in general intelligence, even for London news, they (the London papers) are inferior. Many English Members of Parliament make a point of reading the Scottish papers for better Parliamentary news; and their infinitely better Parliamentary reporting.'

The literary approach of Stoddart's time was catholic, and, in its more extended form concentrated mainly in the Weekly Herald, which during its first ten years (from 1864) had been the inexpensive poor relation, summarising on Saturday 'the news of the week without even a re-setting of the type'. Now, with blossoming ambition it went in for serial stories, though we may doubt if the Editor's own more cultivated and poetic taste was responsible for the gothic choice of 'Moriarty in Exile' and 'The Miser of Haselhow'.

But he was certainly on the selection panel in 1879 when he bought the serial rights for George Meredith's 'The Egoist' for £100. The one snag was that he thought the title was too short, and invoked his editorial prerogative, so that the first instalment appeared under the heading 'Sir Willoughby Patterne, the Egoist'.

The author did not think much of the liberty, and said so in a letter to Robert Louis Stevenson: 'The diplomatic Kegan (his literary agent) has dealt me a stroke. Without a word to me he sold the right of issue of "The Egoist" to the Glasgow Herald, and allowed them to be guilty of a perversion of my title. I wrote to him in incredulous astonishment. He replied to me excusing himself with cool incompetency. He will have to learn – he is but young at it – but these things may be done once – not more.'

Centenary of The Glasgow Herald. *Established 1782.*

The Proprietors request the pleasure of the company of
.... and friend
in the Queen's Rooms on Saturday the twenty eighth instant at 4 p.m.
on the occasion of the
Centenary of The Glasgow Herald.

Herald Office,
Glasgow, 17th January 1882.

The Glasgow Herald celebrated its centenary on the evening and early morning of 27 January 1882. We have already explained the problem of the original files, or rather the lack of them, which led to this miscalculation. The Herald jumped the gun, but it did so handsomely to provide one of the most impressive and roundly resonant occasions of the age in Glasgow.

The intention had been to hold no more than a moderately vainglorious banquet in the Merchants' Hall; but the solicitations were so pressing and numerous that the celebration had to be transferred to 'the ampler accommodation of the St Andrew's Halls', where Fergusson and Forrester of Buchanan Street victualled the 250 guests with a well-watered feast of a dozen courses – with an eight-foot centre-piece on the top table and gilded supporting groups of statuettes of allegorical and classical design. The other table bore 'corresponding plateaux in silver'. As for the company, Parliament, the Kirk, the Seats of Learning, the Civic Institutions, the Armed Forces, the Colleges of Justice, and the Newspaper Press itself, were all capitally represented.

There were 14 toasts, each spoken to ornately and at length, and each replied to with equal opulence; and the company was still reported to have been listening with flattering (and doubtless well comforted) attention, at half-past two in the morning. There were a dozen vintages on the menu.

An invitation to the Herald's first centenary dinner – a year earlier than it should have been because of a misunderstanding. The menu included salmon, roast venison, pheasant and duck, to accompany the 16 toasts.

There was a high voltage inspiration in the air that night, not unconnected with the presence of Sir William Thomson (not yet Lord Kelvin), whose toast to the two Houses of Parliament consisted of a bland, and we guess disinterested, defence of the House of Lords, which he held to be in no need of reform, other than that the Scottish peers (other than elected Representative ones) should be identified by their recognisable Scotch titles. It grieved, and confused, him when the Duke of Argyll had to address his peers as Baron Sundridge, and the Earl of Crawford as Baron Wigan. He also made a passing reference to inventions, which provided a nicely adventitious lead-in for Stoddart, who presided and replied to the toast of the evening. Making his bow to the high priest of electricity, he said: 'Everything seems to be possible to this impalpable and all-pervading force, for not only does it conduct our commercial business, and practically edit our newspapers, but it seems to be the motive power, as well as the material light, of the future.'

Then he went on to make the pertinent reservation that not even electricity can supersede brains '. . . and with whatever little expenditure of them the Newspaper Press may be conducted, I think I may venture to prophesy that they will always remain a factor of some importance in the Press of Great Britain. Brains, I think, also mean freedom – freedom to think, a right which no power on earth can take away, and freedom to speak which alone can make the press valuable. . . . I think I can boast of the Glasgow Herald that during the hundred years of its existence it was never at any time the tool of any party in the State; it never was kept; its advocacy was never bought; its opposition was never sold; its independence and its freedom were never corrupted.' The Herald can claim some fulfilment of his confidence that: 'If the Herald shall last for another hundred years, I am sure that it will last only if it pursues consistently the policy of freedom and independence which has characterised its past history.'

To return to that 'material light', above mentioned, it did not in fact come into Buchanan Street until four years later in 1886, a circumstance explained by Stoddart's fellow-manager, who wrote: 'We started the production of electric light for the sufficient reason that the caseroom, so largely occupied by men, and requiring an unusual quantity of coal gas, soon had its atmosphere in an unwholesome state. The introduction of the new and pure light from electricity was greatly appreciated by the compositors, all of whom reckoned on the enjoyment of better health, and some of them upon greater longevity.'

Newspaper illustration, as we know it now, was still a long way ahead, but in Stoddart's time some progress was made, mainly with the help of a new Pentagraph machine, by which the design was engraved on chalk, included in the type 'chase' and transferred to the stereo plates. The first experiments were made with weather charts, using a skeleton map, with coded squares into which could be translated as isobars the figures telegraphed from the London office. There was an equal success with the reproduction of the scored targets from Bisley.

J.H. Stoddart had a life-long devotion to poetry, which he practised gravely in two substantial published works, and with frequent genial and anonymous satire in the columns of the newspaper. His mother's early instruction, and his own subsequent application gave him the expertise that made him the honorary president of the Glasgow Ballad Club from its beginning in 1876. His own first volume, published by Maclehose in 1879, was 'The Village Life', a recollection of his birth-place and his youth, vivid enough with the 'douce, old, stern, pathetic characters of the old-world Scotch village' – the beadle, the doctor, the schoolmaster, the blacksmith – for the London reviews to applaud it as the 'ripest and most striking book of verse published north of the Border for many years'. His other large later work 'The Seven Sagas of Prehistoric Man' was published in 1884 by Chatto and Windus, and incorporated with imagination and some philosophy much of what he had stored from a lifetime's reading in everything – anthropology, geology, archaeology, and the science of his period. He was also the editor of the second edition of George Outram's 'Legal Lyrics'. Towards the end of his career he was awarded the honorary degree of LL.D. by the University of Glasgow.

As a last word, it seems fair to conclude that James Hastie Stoddart worked himself to death. It was an exhausted man who was sent on an extended health cruise in the Mediterranean, from which he returned in 1888 to die at the comparatively young age for Glasgow Herald editors of 57 years.

Ironclads in their graveyard at a Clydebank breaker's in 1891.

chapter 11

A TALE
OF TWO
OFFICE BOYS

. . . but sail was still in use on the Clyde.
Two steam tugs escort a sailing ship
during the ice of 1895.

AT THIS POINT it may be appropriate to curb what
may seem to be an editorial bias in order to give
their due to two office boys who, consecutively,
kept the ark of Outram not only afloat, but on an
even keel, for 115 years. That may be stretching
the record just a little at both ends, but the
exaggeration is forgivable when we report that
Alexander Sinclair joined the front office in
St Vincent Street, at the age of sixteen, in 1845;
and that Alexander McLean Ewing, having come
into Buchanan Street as a message boy in 1884,
died in Glasgow in 1960 at the age of ninety. Both
came through the ranks to become Director, and
Chairman of the company. One was the founder of
the Press Association, the other was thrice
chairman of that indispensable organisation, as
well as a director of Reuter's Trust. Both wrote
their long experience into the history of these
newspapers.

Alexander Sinclair, aquiline and handsomely
bearded, was remembered as a man who did not
smile much. He was doubtless too busy for such

Glasgow's first horse car to run on rails caused a stir in 1894.
Horse transport was still very popular even twenty years later, as shown by the lower picture of Killermont Terminus.

frivolity; not so much ambitious as always there when he might be needed. 'I grew unconsciously into the several positions occupied by me.'

First he wrote the addresses on the wrappers of the papers and the bundles of papers; and in so fair and fast a hand that soon he was promoted supervisor of a team of 'elderly men called runners', many of them Waterloo veterans, who delivered the Herald to the city and suburban subscribers. As junior clerk he was a noticeable innovator: 'The cashiership fell into my hands because of my early attempts to avoid loss and confusion by having all payments received *entered systematically and at once* instead of trusting to an antiquated practice, which seemed to be a remnant of the old cashier's habit of keeping all the money in his trouser pocket.'

92

By Pagan's time he had already become a managing power on the premises, the arbiter, though it sometimes took some arguing, of technical changes, such as the telegraphs, the rotary presses, the electricity and the stereo printing previously mentioned. As a high-principled commercial manager, he also kept a stern eye on what went into the paper and did not permit advertisements from quack doctors, baby farmers or short 'agony' intimations. For a time he made no direct charge for Births, Deaths and Marriages but instead requested that advertisers made a donation of one shilling to the 'Compositors' Box' which stood on the counter, its contents being handed out in 'driblets' to the printers.

He had shared the frustrations of all the newspaper proprietors for the last ten years of the crippling Advertisement Tax, not to mention

Two views of Glasgow's internationally acclaimed 1901 Exhibition. It marked the Golden Jubilee of the Crystal Palace Great Exhibition of 1851.

the Stamp and Paper Duty, and it was still rankling half-a-century later when he wrote a definitive account of newspaper production in his time, and introduced it, too modestly, as a 'slight record of the important transition period from long enthralment to the boundless freedom now enjoyed by what has been called the Fourth Estate of the Realm'.

It was a freedom, however, about which he had ethical reservations to the end of his day. For example, he never liked the idea of printing the odds on horse-races, which he called 'the chief blot upon newspapers at the present time'. He wrote that the Glasgow Herald would be glad to be rid of the whole thing; but being a realist with always a calculating eye on rivals, he added that to stop giving racing news would just be to encourage 'the bringing into the field of some sporting papers which administer to the lower type of sporting men'.

It has been mentioned that James Pagan was not enamoured of the idea of contents bills. Neither was Alexander Sinclair, but for an even better reason; and he embarked on some very effective propaganda, in the course of which he actually persuaded the proprietors of the Herald's nearest rival to suspend their own operation, which had been on the streets for some time. What he did not say was that Outram had not yet been able to equip themselves with a suitable bill-printing machine and the large wooden type-faces to go with it. When the means arrived, the Herald went into the contents bill business as heartily as any of its competitors.

In the 'seventies of last century, when Sinclair was negotiating the purchase of the new rotary presses, Richard Hoe, from whom he hoped to buy them, forecast that the time was coming when photography would supersede the then up-to-date system of typesetting and machine printing. Sinclair's own gift of prophecy was not quite so reliable, when, about the same time, he also took a look at the latest American invention. 'There is another machine,' he noted, 'an automatic reporter in the form of Edison's phonograph. For reporting purposes, however, while it may some day give aid on special occasions, it is not likely to do the work with the cleanness and efficiency which are given by the discriminating mind and ear of experienced reporters. When made more perfect, these machines may some day be tried in front of speakers; but the Babel of conflicting sounds will prevent such use of them.'

The Herald also owes to him the preservations of some editorial highlights which others have missed. The paper had for example, its own correspondent in the Franco-Prussian War, one Mr DeLifde, who contrived to be present, though not visible, when Napoleon III surrendered to Bismarck after the Battle of Sedan. With another newsman he managed to approach the sloping lawn before the cottage where the meeting was taking place, and, as his despatch to the Herald reported, '. . . the grass being covered with straw I was enabled to throw myself down and see everything that went on'.

The Post Office took over the telegraph companies in 1868. This meant, or would mean, the ending of the news services on which the Herald had been relying since the early 'fifties. In anticipation of this, there was a meeting in Manchester on 28 October 1865, of the four principal provincial newspapers. Alexander Sinclair represented James Pagan for the Herald, James Law represented the Scotsman, and Dr Charles Cameron, the North British Daily Mail. They made themselves a committee to create a company to collect and supply news 'upon a thorough and impartial system, and to promote the interests of their newspapers when the wires were transferred to the Post Office'. And that was the Press Association – with the spin-off of an access to Reuter's foreign service which would cost the subscribers £3000 a year.

Circulation wars have always had their seamy side, and although the Glasgow Herald has never been seriously menaced, Alexander Sinclair as the General Manager had an intimate experience on the receiving end of a remarkable bit of dirty in-fighting. The intended victim was the paper's fledgling stable companion the Evening Times, which was doing too well for the taste of the two other evening papers.

On 10 October 1878, this advertisement appeared in the Evening Citizen and the Evening News: 'Nine tons of Glasgow Evening Times newspapers (about 396,000 copies) for sale as waste, in lots to suit purchasers – Apply 7 Schipka Pass, opposite Gallowgate Station.'

No 7 Schipka Pass was a tiny newsagents' shop, run by a man who had a grudge against the Herald, and 'being poor, he became a tool in the hands of others'. Having first decided to dismiss the advertisement as 'a spiteful squib', Outram then started an investigation; and although a much smaller collection of papers was unearthed, it was revealed that 'a more heterogeneous lot of literature was never, perhaps, before collected. There were copies of papers dead and forgotten years ago, papers from all the principal towns of the United States and Canada, from Victoria, New South Wales, New Zealand, France, Germany, Switzerland and from English towns . . . temperance tracts, missionary records, Choral Union programmes . . . paper table napkins . . .'

The Glasgow Herald reported the investigation, with confessions, on 29 October, to the length of some 4000 words, of which only the last paragraph need be quoted: 'The reader has now the whole conspiracy laid bare. Perhaps he is anxious to learn who Mr T– – – is who was so anxious to make a manufacturing experiment with old newspapers. We are able to identify him. Mr T – – – is the chief reporter, and Mr M – – – is the cashier to Mr F – – – W – – –, proprietor, manager and editor of the Glasgow Evening News.'

The mills of God and of Outram grind slowly, but exceedingly small. The Evening News and the Evening Citizen, which seems to have been privy to the lark, have these many years been absorbed in the Evening Times.

Alexander Sinclair retired from the active management of the papers in 1897, and became a member of the first Board of directors of the private company of George Outram Limited; and as a director he was at the top table for the retirement dinner to Dr Charles Russell, having seen off five editors – Outram, Pagan, Stoddart, Jack and Russell – only one of whom had been a bird of passage.

Alexander McLean Ewing, who might fairly be called a tough customer in business, was anything but austere in his dealings with his colleagues. Indeed at his first (technical) retirement in 1934 there were so many amiable recollections of his staff relations that Sir Robert Bruce – who was never particularly counting house orientated, except in the matter of small advances on his salary, which he frequently sought in the middle of the month, like most of his humbler minions – was moved to say: 'And that is a great thing to say at the end of fifty years of a man who has ever striven after business efficiency, and has never wittingly allowed his heart to lead his head astray.'

Ewing was a bachelor with an appreciative eye in his head, and it may not be irrelevant that under his management the stately mahogany-lined halls of Buchanan Street were always elegantly furnished, particularly behind those counters most convenient to the inquiry and gaze of the public.

The boy, Ewing, new out of Hutcheson's Boys Grammar School and wearing his first long trousers, came into the Herald on his fourteenth birthday 26 May 1884. His passport was a postcard signed by Alexander Sinclair, and it contains a hint of the breadth of the changes that he saw during the succeeding 76 years of his time with Outram, that one of his earliest duties was, each morning, to 'dress' the supply of quill pens that lay on Sinclair's desk. The years brought him other distinction of achievement and decision, but he was undoubtedly the last Glasgow Herald man who knew how to make the diagonal cut and the neat slit in the end tube of firm goose-feathers; and to use his pen-knife for its original purpose. It was, in fact, not until 1896 that the first typewriter was brought into the counting house.

He also had good occasion to remember the first telephone, which was installed just before the General Election in 1885; not only because it gradually relieved him, and other office boys, of running with letters on the simplest matters between business places in the city; but for the initial novelty of overhearing the privileged subscribers – of whom fortunately there were then not too many – ringing up to learn the latest election results. 'After the telephone was introduced,' he recalled, 'I felt rather a grievance. Every time the bell rang, there was always one of the senior men very ready to go and try out the new instrument, and I did not get an opportunity to use it myself. But that only lasted for about a week.'

And he remembered the news that was in the first free copy of the paper that he took home with him. The report of Queen Victoria's 65th birthday and the attempts to get in touch with Chinese Gordon in the Soudan remained as clear as his recollection of being told that his

Swift deliveries are essential to newspapers – and the Mitchell Street headquarters
gave many a circulation manager headaches. Below, Glasgow Bridge at Jamaica Street in 1914.

wages would be £20 a year – when he had been expecting no more than £15.

Ewing, of course, did not take immediate command on the retirement of Alexander Sinclair in 1897. Another general manager intervened (Henry Drummond Robertson); but he was already a decision-maker at the beginning of August 1914 when on the Saturday, news came in of the assassination at Sarajevo. He was then an assistant manager. Both H.D. Robertson and F. Harcourt Kitchin, the Editor of the Herald, were on holiday and incommunicado. On his own immediate responsibility and in consultation with the then Editor of the Evening Times (Michael Graham) it was decided that there must be a special Sunday edition. And while the editorial and printing staffs were alerted to remain on duty, Ewing went to seek out the Chairman of the company at his home in the West End and persuade him that this was the right thing to do. He succeeded so well that the Sunday 'War Times' remained an essential feature of the Glasgow newspaper scene for the succeeding four years.

By 1926 he was in full command, when the General Strike threatened to have the Glasgow Herald off the streets for the first time in 143 years (not counting the single issue that was lost in 1793). Again, in co-operation with the local contemporaries, the reaction was so swift and decisive that the 'Emergency Press' came out of Buchanan Street to fill the bill summarily but adequately until the crisis petered out.

By this time, the Board deferred always to his good advice, and in 1929 and 1930 the expansionist General Manager had his way and re-stocked the Outram stable to the tune of four bi-weekly and weekly newspapers (the Perthshire Advertiser, the Aberdeen Bon Accord, the Mearns Leader and the Angus Herald), the monthly Scottish Field, and the weekly Farming News (which had already swallowed up the North British Agriculturist); not to mention two fully operational and expanding printing works in Perth and Aberdeen; a very advanced facility for lithographic offset printing and full-colour reproduction in Perth; and the goodwill of the Bailie, which for fifty years had been a successful social and literary Glasgow weekly. This, the foundation of the SUN newspapers that now serve the greater part of Scotland, was a good bargain. Ewing was the sole negotiator, and he got the lot for £60,000.

During his last full year as General Manager, he saw the paper's 150th anniversary, and had a constructive part in the editorial celebration of the event.

Just before the start of the First World War, the sole surviving first number of the Glasgow Advertiser came to hand, and this is what he had to say about it: 'Those of you who have seen the original know that there are a great many blanks, and pieces of the text entirely missing. I was very keen to have a reprint of that edition, and I found that in spite of the blanks, I was able to supply every word from newspapers which

In 1930 the Herald was to the forefront in using new technology. Fifty years later it again led the field in switching to full computerisation.

were consulted in Glasgow libraries, in the British Museum and elsewhere. Some of the words were taken from official despatches. . . .' That facsimile, for which a very nearly contemporary type-fount was found, went out with the handsome and exhaustive 150th Anniversary Number. It still turns up from time to time from folk who offer the paper – for a consideration – a specimen of the very first number. Usually however, it is incomplete, having lost the bottom couple of inches off the back page, where an imprint states, clearly but discreetly, just what it is.

Glasgow made more than ships.
Steam Locomotives built by the North
British Locomotive Co., Ltd,
Springburn, are seen being
loaded on the Ellerman Liner 'City of
Barcelona' at Stobcross Quay, Glasgow,
for shipment to Bombay.

When he retired in 1934 Alec Ewing did not sever his connections or relinquish his influence; he joined the Board, where he remained for a further 16 years, ultimately as Chairman. It was in that office, after the war, that the uncompromising quality of his decision-making was remarked when his share of the Glasgow Herald evidence to the Royal Commission on the Press revealed his capacity to defy on principle the importunities of the most powerful but wrong-minded of local advertisers.

At the age of eighty, he resigned from the board, but remained usefully and visibly on the scene putting his long and intimate experience to the good purpose of setting down an administrative history of the Glasgow Herald and the house of Outram, examining with the detail which only he had at his fingertips, the financial structure of the organisation as it developed, through the nineteenth and into the twentieth century, from a one-man undertaking into a complexity of shareholders, trust interests, partnerships, business committees, private limited and then public companies. He came back in 1954 to be fêted on the occasion of the seventieth anniversary of his joining the paper.

On 28 January 1960, he died aged ninety, just a tiny handful of years too soon to observe, if he could not have partaken in, the Fraser-Thomson takeover battle, which would have stimulated his competitive instincts, though it might have been less than pleasing to that sentimental loyalty to the old paper (as an entity and something more than just a property) which along with his heart sat always and decisively on his sleeve.

100

THE BEST LONDON LETTER IN THE COUNTRY

CHARLES GILCHRIST RUSSELL was with the paper 31 years, nineteen of these as Editor. His influence on the Glasgow Herald has been much understated, for it was enormous, and although mainly cultural, it had also been intensely practical.

He succeeded to the chair in 1888, but had been for the whole twelve years of Stoddart's editorship, the Deputy Editor and principal leader-writer. And from the speed with which things began happening once he took over, it is a fair guess that for much of that time he had been nursing and developing ideas which the still tradition-bound partnership were not yet ready to contemplate. When it came to the bit, however, he seems to have been given a free hand. He operated for the first fifteen years of his reign under the unexacting supervision of a business committee which had been appointed some years earlier in an attempt to meet an administrative problem created by the increasing number of absentee partners, most of whom were outsiders – the heirs, representatives and sometimes quite distant relatives of former

THE NEW TAXATION.

IMPOSTS ON LAND.

INCREASES ON SPIRITS AND TOBACCO.

REVISED INCOME-TAX.

LICENSING AND DEATH DUTIES.

1908-1909.

	Estimate.	Result.
Revenue	£154,350,000	£151,578,000
Expenditure	£154,109,000	£152,292,000
Deficit to be met out of Exchequer balances		£714,000

1909-1910.

Revenue on present basis	£148,390,000
Expenditure	164,152,000
Deficiency	£15,762,000
Less new taxation	14,200,000
	£1,562,000

THE ADVANCE UPON LADYSMITH.

BRITISH VICTORY.

BULLER ACROSS TUGELA.

HEAVY FIGHTING SINCE MONDAY.

POSITION CAPTURED BY BRITISH TROOPS.

LORDS ROBERTS AND KITCHENER.

DEPARTURE FOR THE FRONT.

AMERICA CUP.

THE FIRST RACE.

SHAMROCK'S SPLENDID PERFORMANCE.

CHALLENGER LEADS THREE MILES FROM HOME.

TIME LIMIT EXCEEDED.

THE RACE VOID.

FULL DESCRIPTIONS OF THE MATCH.

A RECORD GATHERING OF SPECTATORS.

HOW THE NEWS WAS RECEIVED IN SCOTLAND.

GUN-RUNNING.

GREAT COUP IN ULSTER

50,000 RIFLES LANDED AND CONVEYED INLAND.

PORTION OF THE PROVINCE HELD UP.

COMMUNICATION CUT OFF.

600 MOTOR VEHICLES IN USE.

An extraordinary gun-running exploit was successfully conducted in the north-eastern part of the province of Ulster in the early hours of Saturday morning. The facts read like a chapter from fiction. For coolness

Headlines in their prime – when sub-editors were sometimes required to write up to eight separate headings before the start of a story.

owner-editors and managers. This committee had not much clout, but was useful when technical questions of production arose, needing a timely answer. It had none of the authority of a board of directors (a situation which was put right in 1903).

Russell was the first Editor who had anything approaching a modern notion of the imaginative use of typography, and the first seriously to concern himself with the theory that the appearance of the newspaper might have an effect on its circulation and profitability.

It was a subject upon which he was prepared to lay down the law: 'Why should we huddle our choicest and dearest wares into back pages, and hide them under headings of hardly bigger type than that of the text, as if we were ashamed to show them to our customers?' He did suggest that some American Journals might be going a bit far with 'headlines as high as a five-barred gate', but added: 'A glance at our own old files, and at some newspapers issued now, will show how really repellent a paper may be made to look by an excess of modesty.' He put his theory into practice with stories displayed according to their merit, cross-headings, shortened paragraphs and a wider, and somewhat larger, choice of headline typefaces.

His most ardent belief was in the importance of the leading article which, certainly among his contemporaries, he felt to be in decline. He was not himself long-winded, and his own solution was 'compression without scrappiness', which he achieved by giving the Herald more, but shorter leading articles, and encouraging his staff to look further than only to the most portentous news of the day for subjects worthy of engaging comment.

When Queen Victoria was born in 1819, the Glasgow Herald was a modest 36 years old. Few could have anticipated the impact of her long reign. Two pictures exemplify the dynasty – above, with daughter and grandchildren. Below, her son Edward VII with three future Kings – George V, Edward VIII and George VI – at the Braemar Gathering in 1902.

He did as much for the other columns of the paper, concentrating for a start on the resources of the London office, and extending the content of the London Letter beyond the Parliamentary gossip which had been its staple to include theatre notices, book reviews, movements in society and diplomacy, and observations on the latest developments in the sciences. One cannot feel that he was pitching it too high when he observed this feature with satisfaction and declared it to be the best London Letter in the country.

He also introduced an economical but comprehensive round-up of Continental news. His regard for general news was not less catholic and he successfully made the practical adjustments in such matters as lay-out and tight sub-editing which went some way to meet the not unwelcome problem of '. . . the competition of the various news agencies leading to the discovery or invention by them of varieties of news hitherto undreamt of, which, when once introduced and adopted, are found to be indispensable'.

The abiding impression of Russell's Glasgow as the Glasgow Herald saw it, was literary, artistic – and at one, now significant, stage, architectural. It will wring the withers of today's literary editors – not to mention their alter egos in advertisement departments – to be told that in one issue of the Glasgow Herald, in the '90s, there were 14 columns of book reviews, supported by six columns of publishers' and book-sellers' advertisements.

Then there were the artistic causes that were promoted, against philistine opposition, as when the Glasgow Herald made common cause with the Art Club in 1891 and obliged a reluctant Corporation to buy Whistler's portrait of Thomas Carlyle. Due and exhaustive attention was always given to the Institute of the Fine Arts; and a proprietary interest was taken in the Glasgow School of painters, whom the paper promoted tirelessly. Above all, though at the time the Herald did not know that Mother Outram was suckling a cult figure, there was Charles Rennie Mackintosh. Indeed, had the few succeeding generations of administrators and masters-of-works known what was coming, the Mackintosh corpus might have been spared quite a lot of what the devotees would now denounce as vandalism. And, sale-room prices being what they are, the Herald might have made quite a killing too.

The fact is that although Outram got him to recreate the rear frontage in Mitchell Street and do some interior decorating and furniture-making, a majority in the establishment either did not think all that much of his work, or had never heard of him. When internal alterations were afoot, the first things to go were his partitions with their high, narrow, undustable shelves. The pieces of his furniture which were consigned from office to office until they disappeared, were either uncomfortable, unstable, or both. When the House of Outram flitted from its old home in 1980, all that remained of his originality was the more or less indestructible and peculiar sandstone fenestration and water-tower in Mitchell Street; and, inside, in the old Editor's

An unusual view of
Charles Rennie Mackintosh's exterior
for the Glasgow Herald in 1893.
It was the first major building
he designed.

Charles Rennie Mackintosh
as a young man, and in his maturity.

The Editor's room in Buchanan Street by Charles Rennie Mackintosh, including the ceiling, and the singular stained-glass windows. What is lacking is the original glass-fronted overmantle; the lights are also modern.

room, a brass fireplace canopy, and some *art nouveau* stained-glass windows of a design inspired by the illustration in Gray's Anatomy of the fallopian tubes.

The first redesigner of the Buchanan Street premises in 1870 was the architect John Baird. The next alterations, in 1879, were made by James Sellars, the architect of St Andrew's Halls. When he died in 1888, he was succeeded by his assistant, John Keppie, who went into partnership with John Honeyman; and Charles Rennie Mackintosh was a young member of their professional staff. The major reconstruction of Mitchell Street was commissioned in 1893, and with the Mackintosh hand unmistakably in it, the work continued until 1899.

Charles Gilchrist Russell was an Edinburgh man who had had a variety of early ambitions before he settled on journalism. He went to Edinburgh University with teaching in mind; he dabbled in higher mathematics, and then changed to the medical faculty, from which he dropped out in 1862 to join the Caledonian Mercury as a junior reporter. After two years there, he went to the Leeds Mercury for another two years. He then became literary editor of the Sportsman and after enlarging his general experience as a freelance correspondent to a number of papers, here and abroad, he came north to join Dr Stoddart in 1875. His LL.D. came to him not from Edinburgh but from Glasgow University at the celebration of the 450th anniversary.

In 1903, the inadequacy, and indeed the risks, of the partnership with its unlimited liability, was too apparent to be ignored. A financial reconstruction was put in train and a private limited company was launched, with five of the old business committee as directors. These were Dr Robert Gourlay, James Kennedy, W.R. McGeorge (who would later be succeeded by their own sons), Alexander Sinclair, and as the sixth director James Cameron Dun Waters (whose names recalled three of the old family strains in the organisation). And at that point John Mennons' original £200 capital had multiplied 1500 times into a capitalisation of £300,000.

Like Charles Russell before him, William Wallace has been a somewhat neglected ornament on the Herald's heraldic tabard, mainly, perhaps, because he was the Editor for only three years. But this has been to overlook the fact that he was the Assistant Editor and leader-writer during the whole of Russell's editorship — as indeed Russell himself had been during the whole of Stoddart's incumbency. And he was part and parcel of the more cultivated image which the paper projected then. This was as it should be, for Wallace, anonymous as he was as a daily journalist, was an eminent literateur and scholar, and a biographer of national reputation. Probably his greatest professional admirer was Sir William Robertson Nicoll, the mandarin and oracle of the British Weekly.

It is from the reflection of Wallace's other achievements that his significance in the Glasgow Herald must be deduced. One guess we can make; and that is that his was the inspiration, and almost certainly the writing hand behind the Herald's eloquent advocacy in the campaign to buy Whistler's Carlyle for Glasgow. Carlyle was one of his two choicest subjects; and he contributed the biographical article in 'Chambers' Encyclopaedia', and 'Chambers' Cyclopaedia of English Literature', of which it was said that they stood alone in 'their knowledge, in their ripeness, in their calmness'. His familiarity, indeed, with the Sage of Cheyne Row was such that, as he said himself, he could place any sentence of Carlyle 'after a little thought'.

The other hero was Burns. He produced a monumental 'Life and Works' for Chambers in 1892, followed by an edited edition of the correspondence of Burns and Mrs Dunlop. He was president of the Burns Federation (as was his next successor but one). He was by his writing largely responsible for the preservation of the Auld Brig at Ayr, and for the raising of the money that made the restoration possible. And it was for his work on Burns that St Andrews University conferred his degree of LL.D. He was himself a published historian, and had much more than a passive hand in the foundation of the Chair of Scottish History and Literature at Glasgow University.

He was also responsible, admittedly just before he came to the Herald, for the initial success, if not indeed the 'discovery', of J.M. Barrie. The precise rating of this achievement is for others to judge; but it appears that after touting his manuscript unsuccessfully round the publishers, Barrie at last found a publisher for 'Auld Licht Idylls'. However, when it did appear, 'there were few purchasers, and few reviewers who showed anything like intelligent enthusiasm'. Except, that is, William Wallace, then freelancing on the Spectator. His review pronounced the work to be 'at once the most successful, the must truly literary, and the most realistic attempt that has been made for years, if not for generations, to reproduce humble Scottish life'.

And that was the signal for Barrie and all his works to take off.

William Wallace, when he succeeded to the editorship in 1888, was aged 63, and no longer in the best of health. He came originally from Culross in Fife, where his father, breaking a family tradition in the weaving trade, was the gardener on one of the Rosslyn estates. William, the fifth of a family of promising sons, was a lad of parts who did well at the local school, and, with teaching in mind, took his MA at Aberdeen University.

His only lasting bonus from a brief sojourn as classics master at Ayr Academy, was a burgeoning interest in Robert Burns. The practice of letters was already itching his fingers and inspiring his reading, and he left the schoolroom to become an assistant editor on the Edinburgh Gazette; and remained there only long enough to qualify as Editor of the Dumfries Herald, in succession to Thomas Aird, himself a literary critic, and enthusiast of Burns and Carlyle, and the confidant of the better-known lions of the Blackwoods Magazine hot house. So at Dumfries, according to Robertson Nicoll (a theory which such practitioners are not too fain to endorse), 'The leisure afforded by a country editorship enabled him also to display the literary talent which he practised in abundance.'

He was not a trained reporter, nor was he much interested in politics, but concentrated on special articles, finding his subjects in Scottish history and literature, and, while perfecting his expertise on Burns and Carlyle, extending his catchment area to include such exemplars as Allan Ramsay and Fergusson. With these seeds he sowed the periodical market; and after seven years in Dumfries, he went to London, where he wrote occasionally for The Times, and became a regular contributor to the Spectator. At that time the Herald's London Editor, manager, Parliamentary reporter, and principal writer of the London Letter was James Walker, with whom Wallace struck up a professional acquaintance; and a sufficiently impressive one, so that in 1888, with Russell newly appointed and with lettered intentions for his charge, William Wallace went to Glasgow as Assistant Editor and chief leader-writer.

The productive leisure which we are told he found as a country editor does not seem to have been seriously eroded when he became an editorial executive in Buchanan Street. Much of the felicitous stuff which he turned out for his own satisfaction found its prominent, if unsigned, place in the paper. He had strong views, progressive and a shade libertarian, on the Church and education, which he was free to express in his leading articles. He found time to produce a couple of books of Scottish historical sketches. He remained on the Chambers list of reliable contributors. He had now added Dickens to his scholarship, and with what was reported as an erudite lecture, he inaugurated the Glasgow Dickens Society, of which he became president. He contemplated writing his autobiography; and he was a Justice of the Peace. The only important political decision that was required of him during his three years as Editor was to reassert the Herald's attachment to Free Trade, a lingering controversy which had a few years earlier produced a stimulating local confrontation with Joseph Chamberlain.

It is perhaps illuminating that it was said of William Wallace – and that with no more than a modicum of exaggeration – that during the whole 21 years of his sojourn on the Glasgow Herald, he never once set foot in the caseroom. In 1909, apparently broken in health, he retired. But it was twelve years later, at the age of 77, that he died at his home in University Avenue.

William Wallace, as well as being learned, well-mannered with his pen and exhaustively well-read, was by all reports good humoured – even witty in his generation. At least, he set the table on a roar (at the complimentary staff dinner to Russell) with a fanciful projection to a time when there would be lady reporters on the Herald – and even lady sub-editors. And he had them rolling in the aisles when he went on: 'It would add ten years to my life if every night I could approach some fascinating creation in *mousseline de soie* or *crêpe-de-chine* and say – "My dear Miss A, I should be glad if you would write a sparkling article on the Constitution of the Clyde Trust, or the Bank Rate, or the Unrest in the Balkans." '

It may have been the feeling among the intensely business-minded members of the Board of directors of the swaddling limited company that under the previous two editors, the air of the Herald had become rather too rarified for the mercantile capital of the north. Some such thought must surely have moved them when they sought Wallace's logical successor in London – and thought that they had found him in F. Harcourt Kitchin, the no-nonsense administrator then in charge of the Commercial Supplement of The Times. The experiment was not an unqualified success, though it dragged on for several years. He so far failed to endear himself as to give the impression, even to his most senior assistants, that he had come from London to Glasgow believing that the Herald editorial staff knew nothing about modern journalism. They in their turn believed that they were teaching him; that he was the learner.

The folk-lore of his editorship, therefore, has not been markedly

F.H. Kitchin

109

The Glasgow Herald's office in Fleet Street – packed with sightseers as King George V and Queen Mary travel to a service at St Paul's.

generous. The only recorded episode, indeed, is that he contrived to be on holiday, address unknown, when the First World War broke out. The tale says nothing of how soon he heard the news and hurried back to his desk. All the credit that came out of that crisis week has been reserved for Alexander McL. Ewing, who (as has been mentioned earlier) not only put the Sunday Edition of the Evening Times in train, but had also had the anticipation to place an early order with the Donside Paper Mills, and to follow it up with an arrangement which ensured that Outram did not suffer seriously from a lack of newsprint during the rest of the war.

In 1917, Harcourt Kitchin went back to London to edit the Board of Trade Journal; and when asked why he had decided to leave the Glasgow Herald he replied that he was doing so because he feared that if he remained any longer his children would be growing up to speak with a Glasgow accent. There were others as uncharitable as his immediate colleagues. When he went, and the name of his successor was announced, the Bailie headed its 'Monday Gossip' column with the paragraph: 'Scottish history for Glasgow journalists: William Wallace, the English interregnum, Robert Bruce.'

110

BRUCE IN BUCHANAN STREET

ROBERT BRUCE was a round, brisk, accomplished little man; and as vain as he had good occasion to be – a knighthood (albeit a Lloyd George one) and three LL.D.'s can be accounted a sufficient quiverful to be going on with. He was essentially a Parliamentary journalist, an intuitive news-getter, and an often and discreetly rewarded respecter of confidences. He was a prime exemplar of the man who stayed long enough in one place (in his case, nineteen years in the corridors of Westminster) to consolidate the continuing, fruitful connections. By the time that he came to Glasgow, young politicians whom he had grown up with in the Lobbies had become statesmen; and his own reliability kept him intimately in their counsels, and with unparalleled access to their intelligence.

Sir Robert Bruce

His successor, but then his deputy, William Robieson, told how in 1932, which was eighteen years after he had left London, Bruce paid a routine visit to the London office. The talking point at that time was tariffs, and the political

111

correspondents on the spot, delve as they might, had failed to discover who was to be the Chairman of the Imports Duties Advisory Committee. Bruce had gone to London on the morning train; by mid-evening he was on the telephone to his deputy in Glasgow, saying: 'The first paragraph of the London Letter will announce who is to be Chairman of the Advisory Committee. No other paper will have it but one, and they will have it because I have told their Parliamentary Correspondent.'

That is but one example of many, the sort of thing that happened when he paid fleeting visits to his old stamping ground. And indeed, at long distance the telephone was just as productive, for, in both the senses of the word, Downing Street had his number.

Bruce was probably the most exclusively editorial of all the Herald's earlier chiefs. Though he conceded, when pressed, the usefulness of advertisements for paying the salaries of himself and his staff, the burden of his argument was always: 'It is the news that sells the paper.' His was the only white-painted door on the premises – a sort of celestial third-floor portal upon which managers and directors from the lower floors knocked and awaited permission to speak, just like everybody else. And although he was for twenty years the most dominant personality in the establishment, he was never invited to join the Board of directors of the company.

This was an oversight for which domestic legend in Buchanan Street has long assigned probable cause. In 1918, just one year after his appointment as Editor of the Herald, it seems to have been hinted that, with his old and close acquaintanceship with Lloyd George, he might be the perfect intermediary to solicit a knighthood for the Chairman of the Outram Board. It would appear, however, that the Prime Minister, co-operative as always, had either misheard or misunderstood his old friend's advocacy. The official message that did come announced that 'His Majesty has been pleased to approve the recommendation of the Prime Minister that Robert Bruce should receive a knighthood.'

Sir Robert did insist that the honour had come to him totally unexpectedly. However, some wisps of substance may be assigned to the myth from the fact that, by his own report, the next Editor, William Robieson, when about to take office, was instructed that should he ever be offered a knighthood, he was not to accept it without the express permission of the Board. That, in the event, was a requirement which lapsed, since Sir William got his knighthood as a member of the Royal Commission on Population upon which he sat for several years following the Second World War.

Robert Bruce was a native of Alloa, and when he left school at the age of 15 he joined the Alloa Advertiser as the office boy, but not for long. He was soon broken-in to the comprehensive school of general reporting which used to, and hopefully still does, provide that grounding to future accomplishment which was best laid in the weekly country newspapers. At 21, he went to the Aberdeen Journal, where

Family holiday pictures always
tell a story – sometimes not the one
intended. These two station scenes
of Glasgow departures for the coast
are vivid examples. The barefoot,
ragged boy on the right of the
scene above (1910) was carefully
excluded from the published picture.
The scene below (c1914) gives an
interesting contrast between two
boys – the one awaiting his train, the
other collecting tickets.

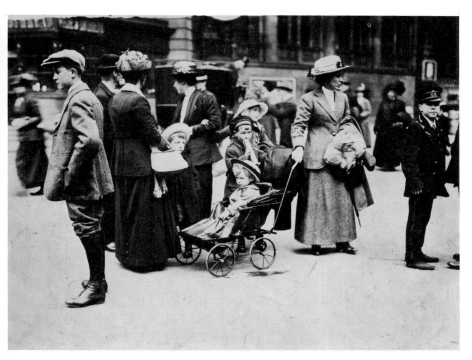

This classic picture shows three boys –
in 1913 being barefit was the rule
rather than the exception – enjoying
an unauthorised paddle behind a
Glasgow city watercart. It was
published by the Glasgow Herald, but
originally a prize-winning picture
taken by Mr William Fraser of its
sister paper the Bulletin. His camera:
a £9 second-hand Thornton-Pickard.

he got his first taste of, and for, political reporting, a line which he
pursued with such diligence that he was sent south to handle the
London correspondence with a particular remit to Parliament.

There he made contact with the Glasgow Herald – to which he had
unsuccessfully applied for a job as a reporter while he was still in
Aberdeen – and in 1898 he was taken on as a member of the Parliamentary staff. We must conclude that the prestige of the position
compensated for its financial limitations. In those days, Gallery reporters were paid only while Parliament was sitting; and that was seldom
for more than 26 weeks in the year. Bruce never made much of how he
managed during the other, straitened, six months, speaking only of
one modest subvention. In those days frock-coats were *de rigeur* for
journalists at Westminster; frock-coats and, of course, tile hats. When
wear and tear, and the douce Glasgow Herald image, dictated a
replacement – though we doubt if he got it on expenses – our embryo

114

West George Street, Glasgow, in the
1920's. Below, Union Street in 1955.

Editor sold his discarded tiles for sixpence to a Fleet Street hansom cabby who varnished them and gave them another lease of use.

In the Houses of Parliament, Bruce laid the foundations of his distinguished editorial career, developing those talents of resource, and the nose for not-immediately-obvious news which by 1905 had already made him one of the leading political journalists of his day. He became progressively Gallery reporter, sketch-writer, Lobby correspondent and London Editor of the Herald. His polished timing, and the clear judgment which seemed always to place him in the right place to hear the right whisper at the right time, was exhibited in the London Letter, most of which he wrote himself. And the Letter was required, if sometimes disconcerting, reading in the Palace of Westminster.

One example of his talent for reaching the right conclusion, and being brave enough to exploit it, dates from the first year after he joined the Herald. We have it in his own words, as he quoted it, nearly forty years later for the instruction of successors in the art of putting

Tanks, a relatively new weapon of warfare, caused intense interest in Glasgow, 1917. They were less welcome in the city two years later (below) when they returned after the 1919 strike.

two and two together. Thus: 'Picture a dull night in the House of Commons. It was a Foreign Office night. George Nathaniel Curzon was the solitary occupant of the Treasury Bench. There was nothing doing in the Lobby, and I was sitting in the Gallery in a brown study. I became alert. A back-bencher walked down the gangway and slapped

Open air pleasures for rich and poor alike – above, a grouse-shooting party in the 1920's, below, a street Punch and Judy show at the corner of Rose Street and Sauchiehall Street in the early years of the century.

George Nathaniel on the shoulder. George Nathaniel, who never permitted liberties, smiled. Then another obscure back-bencher hurried down and seized his hand. Again, there was a smile. I pondered, and then wrote that George Nathaniel Curzon had been appointed Viceroy of India. The official announcement did not appear until a week later.'

He was a master, too, of the less speculative techniques of his trade. For example, in the matter of State funerals he was something of a connoisseur. He reported these at length, an assignment that called only for some enlargement, with more panoply, of those descriptive skills which he had begun picking up as a junior reporter around the humbler sepulchres of Alloa. He covered the funeral procession of Queen Victoria through London, and he was the Herald's reporter inside St George's Chapel, Windsor, at the burial of Edward VII, at whose coronation he had been the outside observer of street scenes. But he was the Herald's man inside Westminster Abbey for the coronation of George V.

In June 1914, Robert Bruce had been appointed Assistant Editor, but he did not make the transition to Glasgow until after the outbreak of war. Now the political skills of the report were welded into the critical and opinionated demands of leader-writing, a task, however,

The Red Flag in George Square during the strike in 1919 for a 40-hour week. It led to riots and the subsequent trial of (left to right) Emmanuel Shinwell (5 months), William Gallacher (3 months), George Ebury (not guilty), David Brennan (not guilty), David Kirkwood (not guilty), Harry Hopkins (not guilty) and James Murray (3 months).

which did not daunt him. And, administratively, he had to react to the multiplied problems that came with the war. The shortage of news-print made the paper much smaller, and this had its inverse effect upon a critically reduced staff. This was particularly so in the case of the sub-editors, who were required to find a new expertise in condens-ing; a difficulty that had not been burdensome in the lavish tradition of long columns, and near-verbatim reporting of every aside from every public platform.

Even the immediate feature of war news suffered from the lack, until much later, of the descriptive war-correspondents who had dramatised the Boer War. The only reporting allowed from the front line was anything but exclusive, for it came from the official War Office 'Eyewitness' – and that military official was the forerunner to the Public Relations Officer of the Second World War, who was never the most highly regarded collaborator of the individual newspaper journalists on any front from France to Burma. For a time, the uniform despatches of the 'Eyewitness' were filled out and coloured with extracts from the letters that the soldiers wrote home. This had been an invaluable staple to the newspapers since the time of Waterloo. Trench warfare and a strict censorship put an end to that. When in action the ordinary soldier's only permitted correspondence was a pro-forma postcard with a space for his signature below two or three categories of printed alternatives, to be ticked off or scored out accord-ing to their nearest approximation to his state of health and his degree of cheerfulness. In the later campaigns war-correspondents were allowed forward, and two of these, Martin Donohoe and George Renwick, were shared by the Herald.

Robert Bruce's local indoctrination was complete by the time, in 1917, that Harcourt Kitchin reckoned he had had enough of Glasgow. And though from then on Bruce threw himself into the organisation and editorial development of his paper, he retained to the end a nostal-gia for his brave days in the Mother of Parliaments. He made the most of one engaging coincidence, and was never blate to point out that, exactly from the day he left London for Glasgow, Big Ben did not boom again for four years.

After the war, there came stirring political times in these parts, starting with the Red Clyde, when Bruce, taking an independent line for such a sometimes conformist newspaper, resisted the clamour for a return to the older party politics, and urged instead a continuation of the Coalition of the Conservatives and the Lloyd George Liberals in the expectation that this would stem the rising Labour tide. Not that he denied all virtue to the demagogues of the purlieus of George Square and the Red Clyde. This came, admittedly a little later, when personal passions were cooling, but one of his leading articles is on record as saying that 'to call Emmanuel Shinwell an extremist is, perhaps, to do him an injustice'.

We have mentioned one of Sir Robert's scoops, but to illustrate his undiminished sagacity and self-confidence in this unchancy competition, we may cite two others, more than thirty years apart. At the beginning of this century a matter of intense (and intensely worldly) interest was exciting the nominally pious majority in Scotland. This was the Free Church Case, following the schism caused by the union of the bulk of the Disruption Free Church with the United Presbyterians, to form the United Free Church. After repeated litigation, which reached the House of Lords, a rump of fewer than a dozen Highland ministers were declared to be the sole legal inheritors of all the property of the original church – including a college, a great library, an Assembly Hall on the Mound of Edinburgh, a fortune in funds, and a domain of church buildings stretching from the Pentland Firth to the Solway. It took an Act of Parliament to redistribute the property, to the satisfaction of the United Frees, and to the enduring lamentation of the Wee Frees.

The reallocation was in the hands of the Elgin Commission, whose report was awaited with anxiety and impatience. No forecast of its contents was leaking. Then one day an unsigned single sheet of paper was furtively slipped into Bruce's pocket. Its half dozen lines of writing gave the gist of the findings.

Let Bruce tell the rest himself: 'One essential date was missing. A great deal hung upon that date. But I had been through the proceedings, and I plunged for one day, which turned out to be right. Dr Russell was then the Editor. I sent a message over the wire asking him to splash the story and not to inquire as to my source of information.' The splash, which the story got, amounted in those days to a double-column heading at the top of the main news page – not the front page, which was sacred to Births, Deaths and Marriages, but the right-hand middle page, opposite the leaders. 'There was a great commotion among the Church people, and from a few of them some abuse; but three or four weeks later, the Herald was acclaimed as an intelligent anticipator of coming events.'

The most prestigious 'beat' came in the early '30s. During the Depression, when the building of the Cunarder 534 was suspended, Sir Robert, for reasons not unconnected with his political standing, was invited to act as intermediary between John Brown's and Cunard and the Government. A year or two later, in the wake of a premature flush of confidence, the agencies circulated a circumstantial report that the building of the Cunarder would restart almost immediately. Front page news! The Herald would have used it, too, except that in the course of the evening, Sir Robert received a personal telephone call. The result was that next day the Glasgow Herald was the only national daily newspaper without the story. It suffered a bit of insincere sympathy in consequence.

But the Cunarder did not restart – then. When it did, the Herald had the news to itself – at least in the first edition. The prelude to that was another personal call to Bruce '... to authorise you exclusively to

The Queen Mary leaving the Clyde
to start her long career . . .
the Herald had a world scoop
when she was still Cunarder 534.

announce tomorrow morning that the work on the Cunarder will be resumed on Monday'. That was the Queen Mary; and the scoop was the spin-off of the practical diplomacy that moved a former Chancellor of the Exchequer (inevitably another old friend) to praise Sir Robert as 'the trusted confidant of statesmen and the sagacious adviser of many business men'.

Like all great men Robert Bruce had his blind spots. He was not always entirely up to date in foreign matters. His metier was domestic affairs; with a team of more generally informed leader-writers and correspondents to direct their eye and their assessment to what was going on abroad. Where these affairs impinged upon British Parliamentary thinking, then he was himself the only interpreter. But he did not charge his mind excessively with petty detail. Thus: it used to be the custom in the Herald's leading articles to print all personal names in capital letters. At the time of Mussolini's conquest of Ethiopia, a leader-writer wrote something to the effect that 'Addis Ababa reports . . . .' When the proof arrived on the Editor's desk, with the words in caps and lower case, he was heard to mutter 'Careless!' as he uncapped his fountain pen and added the three underscored lines that turned the town into a person.

Sir Robert Bruce had the gift of friendship, but it could be capricious.

121

Jarrow marchers halt for tea
on their long trek to London in 1936.

John Buchan (Lord Tweedsmuir)

This never hurt anybody, but it could be disconcerting to his staff, and especially to his literary editor. One of the longest lasting objects of his regard, but not uncritically, was John Buchan. It was only to be expected therefore, and perfectly justified by the merit and popularity of the work, that his newest novel should be reviewed at length, enthusiastically; and prominently displayed on the Book Page. The Literary Editor, however, was summoned to the presence, and smartly lectured upon the inferior judgment that could give such effusive and overlong treatment to what was after all just a rollicking adventure story. What Sir Robert did not mention was that he had temporarily fallen out with his old crony.

The chastened underling, who could take a hint as discreetly as anyone else, kept a weather eye open for the next Buchan book; and when it came did not commission a review but himself wrote a short, descriptive and polite, but undemonstrative quarter-column, and placed it down the page. He was summoned again to hear a similar dressing down for poor judgment. This time it was the poor judgment that had given such a miserable little notice to the latest work of our leading Scottish novelist. It is hardly necessary to mention that in the meantime, the friendship had resumed its earlier and continuing warmth.

Sir Robert made his own excursion into hardback. The title was 'Greystones', and it was written, however unconsciously, under the influence of the John Buchan style. There was a distinctly patrician 'John McNab' flavour to it. This book would be hard to come by today, but it was fully familiar to the more or less senior members of his staff, who used to be detained after the editorial conference as a captive audience to a reading of each chapter as it was finished. This book was reminiscent, episodic, and grown out of the soil of his own professional

122

life. The setting was a week-end country cottage, where a company of the topmost men in their callings, well-dined, their tobacco-pipes drawing sweetly, relaxed while turn about each of them tell a story. The bones of each of these might have been identified by a diligent searcher in the files of twenty years of London Letters. It was a competent early exercise in what is now called 'faction'.

No one could but say that Robert Bruce was instinctively old-fashioned, with an established sense of the proper priorities; yet his willingness to move with the times is patent in this announcement that appeared, not too prominently, on 1 February 1919: 'An article on topics of interest to women is given today. It will appear weekly.' And he lived to see it, and no doubt to read it too, not weekly but daily.

It is a defect in the Herald's records that, apart from the editors and a few managers and partners, they have so little to tell us about the minor actors in the long-running pageant. Indeed the only early bit-player who has been sketched in was the Flea, the printer who in the middle of last century was hailed before the General Assembly of the Free Church for helping to compose the Glasgow Herald on the Sabbath. But we are now drawing towards living memory, and to the recollection of other individualists who belonged to the Bruce era, some of whom survived to lend colour to the reigns of his successors.

Of these the first that comes to mind is Willie Doleman, the editorial messenger, the holder of an office infinitely more important than it sounds. This functionary was (indeed still is) the man who stands guard by the pnuematic tubes, where he receives the agency and other messages, classifies them, and distributes them to the appropriate specialist desks. His skill, and restraint, measures the difference between a steady and manageable flow of copy and a discouraging mountain of agency flimsies on the sub-editor's desk.

The relationship between Doleman and Bruce was primevally Scotch. To Doleman, Bruce was just another, albeit an important, member of the editorial staff who needed looking after, while the Editor tacitly acknowledged the independence and indispensability of the editorial messenger – who always went his own way without dissembling. They collaborated without condescension and without servility; but with a mutual understanding.

Between editions, round about nine o'clock, the staff dispersed to its various places of nourishment; Bruce to dine at the Western Club, Doleman to make his way either to Samuel Dow's or the Horseshoe Bar. Neither, as a rule, stinted himself. On the general return to the desks, two bells was the summons for the messenger to collect the galley proofs that had accumulated in the absence and carry them through the white door. On one such night, the proofs trailing from him like bunting, Willie tacked his insecure way through the furniture of the sub-editors' room; and on his equally erratic return he paused by the foreign sub's desk to confide: 'He's weel gassed the nicht.' An exaggeration, we have no doubt; but artist as he was himself in con-

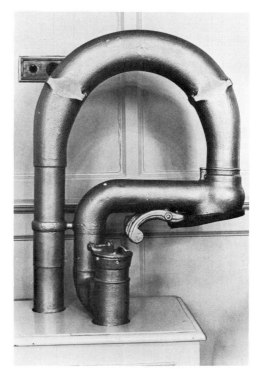

This pneumatic tube graced the Editor's room in Buchanan Street. Into its sometimes capricious maw would be placed the leaders of the day – to be returned with a dull thump in proof form. Its use was banned in the 1950's after an important leader became lost in the system and had to be re-written, holding up the paper. After this episode, carbon copies were also made mandatory.

viviality, he was a shrewd observer of the moods of editors, and frequently operated as a valuable early-warning system.

Then there was the 'Byre', an unpretentious sanctum at the end of a long corridor, with a vast and authoritative output dedicated to agriculture and music. We know little of that music critic, save that his name was Robert Turnbull. But James Cameron, a magisterial presence with a pointed grey beard, was the last word on dairy cows and farming politics. He was a judge at national shows; and he used to be called in as arbiter in disputed judgments. In the paper he could wax lyrical about an Ayrshire cow 'with a grand top line and very sweet about the tail'; though it was his successor in office, William Adair, who invoked Solomon and called the Aberdeen Angus 'the black but comely breed'.

Even in 1930 the Highland Show was a major agricultural event. The 1925 picture below shows rabbits being judged as a class for the first time, with the Earl of Elgin (left) lending a paternal presence.

When it came to the Highland and the English Royal Shows which for two generations were covered with massive and definitive supplements – James Cameron had the whole resources of the reporting staff, and the district offices, at his command. This was an assignment which over the years bred quite a few specialists, two of whom in their turn became Agricultural Editor. The first of these was Adair, who was a general reporter in 1909 and covered the trial of Oscar Slater. When he concentrated on farming he became an acknowledged expert on Clydesdales; and his is the best and fullest account of that enchanting dispute of Dunlop and Kirkpatrick (or rather, Dunure and Craigie Mains) over the ownership of Baron of Buchlyvie, the greatest of stallions.

Nowhere was the dignity and the privilege of the Glasgow Herald more single-mindedly cherished than in the reporters' room, under the unforgiving eye of James Robertson, who insisted that his reporters attend public dinners in full evening dress. The sound of the door to his little room being slammed shut with an indignant back-heel as he passed through was the sure sign that he had just noticed one of his staff wearing merely a dinner-jacket. His reporters were also under instruction that, should they be treated with less than due respect in the matter of table placing – that is, if they were relegated to a side room to await the start of the speeches – they were to leave at once without taking a note.

James Robertson, a Fifer, was a modest Gaelic scholar, in that he read and wrote the language easily. But it was a constant pain to him that when he tried it conversationally on Peter the Hoist, originally from the craggier parts of north-west Perthshire, that bi-lingual, unlettered and insufferable old Highlander would reply: 'It would be better if you would just speak to me in the English, Mr Robertson. That way I will be able to follow what you are saying.'

As for note-taking, the dictator and shepherd was Bob Murchie, the

Some ideas are half-a-century ahead of their time – but they live on the Herald's vast picture library. Left, the Bennie railplane at Milngavie; below, a motorscooter of 1919 vintage.

deputy chief, who organised his verbatim teams in pairs of reporters doing two-minute 'takes'. He took the check note himself, and reckoned that by his method, and with an agile relay of runners, the main speeches could be in type and on the street while the vote of thanks was still being spoken.

His own shorthand was extremely fast. It is said that he was beaten only once, and that a packed audience in St Andrew's Hall was made aware of it. The most mercurial speaker of his day was Lord Rosebery who had a delivery rate of something just short of two hundred words a minute. And there was Murchie at the reporters' table below the platform, keeping up splendidly, until his Lordship raced on into an extended Latin quotation. At this the enraged reporter sat back in his chair, hurled his pencil at his open notebook, and cried, so that all the audience might hear 'The bugger!'

The nearest approach the Herald then had to an outer space correspondent was a diminutive and sometimes irascible person known to the staff as Sun, Moon and Stars. His name was J.J. Ross. He was no Patrick Moore, and he comes to mind now only because Percy Gordon,

No press photographer is able to resist pretty girls splashing about on the beach. These two pictures (above, 1928, below, 1937) show how styles in beachwear changed in nine years.

(Opposite, right)
Scotland wins rugby's Triple Crown by beating England at Twickenham in 1938 by five tries to one – a match (and a man) that will long be remembered. Here R. Wilson Shaw, Scottish captain and stand-off half, has evaded the tackle by the English full-back to score the first of his two tries. His second, minutes before full time, came after a dazzling run which split the English defence and ended with Shaw diving full length over the goal line. Scottish supporters carried him shoulder-high from the pitch at the end of the match, which was watched by King George and Queen Elizabeth, the first occasion on which a Queen had visited Twickenham.

the music critic, himself no giant, said of him, 'How presumptious in so small a man to write about the Universe.'

One of the innovations of the early 'twenties, along with Women's Topics, was the Week-end Page, the forerunner of the now enlarged Saturday feature. We know who some of the early contributors were, such as J.J. Bell and Professor J. Arthur Thomson, who wrote regularly and popularly about science and new discovery. But for the rest no clue remains except the occasional initials at the end of an article. The names came much later, for it was not until the late 'fifties that the Herald at last followed the herd and adopted by-lines, there and throughout the paper. The Week-end Page disappeared only between 1942 and 1946, when the shortage of newsprint cut space.

Between the wars, the Herald editorial staff was not as compartmented as it has become. Leader-writers looked after the special articles and the Week-end Page. There was no Features Department as such. Even sport was managed by one specialist sub-editor and a panel of volunteers. And except on rare special occasions, the Monday night theatre notices were a prerequisite of the reporters' room, and these threw up such odd purple passages as 'The spontaneous

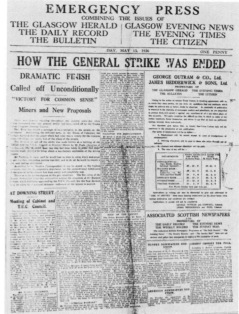

EMERGENCY PRESS
COMBINING THE ISSUES OF
THE GLASGOW HERALD | GLASGOW EVENING NEWS
THE DAILY RECORD | THE EVENING TIMES
THE BULLETIN | THE CITIZEN
DAY, MAY 13, 1926 ONE PENNY

salute of approbation that greeted the fall of the curtain last night at the King's Theatre. . . .'

During the General Strike Sir Robert Bruce edited the four-page Emergency Press in Glasgow, which is said to have had a circulation of more than a quarter of a million. Towards the end of his newspaper career he presided over the 150th anniversary of the Glasgow Herald, and then in the winter of 1936 he retired to become a director of the London Midland and Scottish Railway Company, a distinction which carried with it the most privileged prerequisite of a little gold medallion to hang on his watch chain.

A Glasgow bus overturned during the General Strike in 1926. During the strike six papers combined to produce the Emergency Press.

Classic days of swing . . . Above, Bobby Jones in his heyday, having won the British Amateur and Open and then the US Amateur and Open. Right, Sheila Stroyan, the Scottish captain, tees off at Stoke Poges in the first Girls' International between Scotland and England in 1938 (Scotland won 4-3). Opposite page, Bobby Jones is granted the freedom of St Andrews in 1958.

This badge was the open sesame to every railway system between Wick and Istanbul; and when he flicked it to the respectful notice of inspectors and ticket collectors, it may be wondered if he recalled the time, forty years earlier, on the Aberdeen Journal when he was sent (on a 'facility') to do a special article on the railway in the north-east province. He had reached Cairnie Junction on his tour, and was sitting in a carriage full of Buchan farmers when the door opened and a forbiddingly bearded station-master demanded 'Tickets, please.' The reporter was the last to be inspected, and he handed over his special, folded, document.

'Fit's this?' inquired the railwayman, fishing in his pocket for his steel-rimmed specs, which he balanced carefully on his nose before opening the paper and reading, slowly, and aloud every word:

GREAT NORTH OF SCOTLAND RAILWAY COMPANY

Pass the Bearer, Robert Bruce,
on all stations of the
Great North of Scotland Railway.

Signed: *John Gordon, General Manager*

He folded the *laissez-passer* as carefully and as slowly, and returned it, saying: 'Aye, aye. Gey chape traivlin!'

128

The most important fiscal transaction of the period was the decision, in 1919, to register Outram as a public company. In January of that year, an extraordinary meeting of the shareholders agreed that: 'From a reserve fund of £160,000 a sum of £120,000 be withdrawn and added to the capital of the company; that there be created twelve hundred Six-and-a-half percent Redeemable Preference shares of one hundred pounds each, and that these shares be issued as a capital bonus to the

The music hall and pantomime played a front part in Glasgow social life before the advent of television. Jack (Hilary Allan) is seen at the Alhambra in 1941, showing the magic beans to Harry Gordon and Will Fyffe.

members in the proportion of £1000 of the new preference stock for each share of £2500 held by the member. And further that the one hundred and twenty ordinary shares of the company of a nominal value of £2500 should become three thousand shares of one hundred pounds each.'

The issued capital was now £420,000, and at the formation of the new company, a large number of shares were given as a free gift to members of the Outram staff. By the end of 1926, the issued capital of the company amounted to £876,000.

King George VI and Queen Elizabeth at
Ballater in 1937 with Lord Aberdeen
and Colonel Duff of Hatton. The present
Queen (only Princess Margaret's legs
are visible) is on the left.

131

chapter 14

AND SO TO MUNICH

Sir William Robieson

ALTHOUGH HE WAS the obvious choice for the job, having been for ten years Assistant Editor and chief leader-writer to Bruce, William Dunkeld Robieson passed the first phase of his distinguished editorship under close supervision.

About this time the Editor of the Evening Times had also reached retiring age; but when Sir Robert Bruce left to lend his presence to the councils of the railway company, James Willock remained on the premises, and on the board, in the new office of Editorial Director. He moved upstairs to share the Mackintosh room with the new Editor; and he had his own desk, behind the door, from which (usually silently) he observed editorial conferences, and the more casual discussions that took place throughout the day. But he seldom remained after the late afternoon leader-writers' conference. After 46 years on the evening paper, he was accustomed to going home before dusk.

Whatever original doubts may have been implicit in these arrangements, these were soon enough seen to be patently unfounded as

Robieson, entering what was to be the most commanding period in the paper's history, was more than a master of those recurrent crises where censorship, depleted staffs and newsprint shortage in a less composed man might have induced panic and indecision. The run-up to the war was already under way in 1936, with Mussolini in Abyssinia, Francisco Franco in Spain, Adolf Hitler threatening soon to be everywhere else. There was, of course, the superficial display of confidence in 1938 when for six months the Empire Exhibition, at Bellahouston, made a colourful diversion for some – indeed for a great many – while Hitler was making his final, quasi-diplomatic preparations for the rape of Czechoslovakia.

Robieson's capacity to be uncompromising in principle, with the courage to stand out alone against the flood of euphoria that swept the country under the magic wand of Chamberlain's umbrella, has provided the Herald with its most valued demonstration of steadfast

Peace in our time . . .
Mr Neville Chamberlain arriving back at Heston Aerodrome after his talks with Hitler on the Czechoslovakian crisis. The Herald was not impressed, and denounced the Munich Agreement.

Alexander McL. Ewing

independence under pressure. There were at that time some very important people who felt that Hitler and all his works were not such a bad thing. The Herald was otherwise minded, and said so bluntly in a leading article that denounced the Munich Agreement and the policy of appeasement.

And for the first time in its history the Herald came under open pressure from the Government, and from attempted blackmail by captains of industry (or at least one, and in this area, the most powerful of them). How the paper stood up to them is on public record (ten years later) in the evidence given before the Royal Commission on the Press. As a reaction to that leader and to other editorial comments, William Robieson and Alexander Ewing (in his capacity as a director of the company) were summoned to London to be disciplined by a member of the Cabinet; not, as it was pointed out, the Foreign Minister, but one speaking on his behalf.

Here Robieson is answering a leading question from a member of the Royal Commission:

> ... He made it quite clear that while he and his colleagues thought that our shortcomings were due to a lack of information, they were undoubtedly shortcomings. We thanked him and said we took note of what he had said. That is the only case in which any member of any Government has asked us to see him and has made it clear that they dislike the line we have taken.

The Herald continued the line that had been taken, and was, of course proved right. But to continue with the evidence, and the local side-effects:

> *Chairman:* When you went on taking more or less the same line ... was there any decline in your advertisements as a result during that period?
>
> *Robieson:* No.
>
> *A Commissioner:* You issue an Annual Trade Review in which all the shipping companies advertise. Was there a decline in the advertisements to the extent that your advertising manager approached some of these shipping people and asked for the reason and was ultimately told that it was due to the articles in the Glasgow Herald on Munich?
>
> *Ewing:* There was an indication at one stage that our policy did not please the chairman of a large commercial organisation, and he was responsible for cancelling one or two advertisements for companies in which he was concerned, but our advertising manager saw him and asked if it was because of the attitudes of the Glasgow Herald on any political matter that those advertisements were being withdrawn, because if it were, we would publish the fact that he had withdrawn the advertisements under

134

pressure from someone else. . . . There were no advertisements cancelled; it was just one of those instances where a man thinks he can, by threatening to withdraw advertising, effect his purpose; but I am certain he saw the error of his ways and there was no cancellation.

Commissioner: Would you care to name the individual?

Ewing: No, I would not like to.

Chairman: We have been informed that certain people have tried to bring pressure to bear on the Press of this country. . . . I was anxious to get that information because I think it very important that no Government should interfere with the press of this country, and I want to say in the presence of Sir William Robieson and Mr Ewing that the Glasgow Herald has come out of this question with flying colours; but I did have information that pressure was brought to bear and my point is that perhaps some other paper would not have been able to take the stand that you took.

William Robieson was a twin son of the schoolmaster of Fossoway in Kinross-shire. He went to Dollar Academy and to Glasgow University, where he took a first class honours degree in History. After a year abroad doing historical research he returned to become assistant to the Professor of History at Glasgow. It was indeed as a lecturer that he shone, in the sense that none has matched him in the lucid, exhaustive and impeccably balanced briefing that he gave for twenty years to his writing staff. Curiously, though he wrote excellently, he did not particularly enjoy writing. And he once confessed that during the fifteen years with Bruce, when he turned out a leader nearly every working night, he always looked forward to a time when he might be spared that daily stint. As Editor, of course, he wrote, but highly selectively and rarely, on the subjects of his specialised experience and scholarship.

And that scholarship was vast and meticulous. Here is one of his earlier colleagues on that talent which he applied to the instruction of his younger colleagues: 'An adept in discussion; most reasonable in argument. I have never met anyone so full of facts. He sets them out in orderly rows before one's astonished gaze. His command of the tools and the materials of his trade is quite remarkable. Ask him a question, and before you can say "knife" he is pouring out a leading article. The date of the Battle of Hastings is remembered by most of us, but Bill Robieson can tell you what the weather was like, the number of arrows expended, and what the sergeant said when he sat on a spike.'

The Herald's London office being sandbagged in 1940.

It is characteristic of scoops, more particularly in wartime, that they tend to exist only in the imagination of the newspapers that claim them. Censorship sees to that; and one of the clearest examples of this is to be found in the case of Rudolf Hess, who parachuted out of a Messerschmitt on the evening of Saturday, 10 May 1941, and landed, with a hurt ankle, on a field at Floors Farm, near Eaglesham.

That is a story that is in no need of retelling. But the fact is that the public first got the news, the detail and the interviews, in all their newspapers on the morning of the Tuesday. The private satisfactions about the scoop — and these have enjoyed some exaggeration during the past forty years — lies in bragging about who first knew the identity of the visitor — before the Herald was allowed to publish it. Claims in this regard are cherished in the folk-lore of the Daily Record and the Scottish Daily Express. What really happened of course — and this is

The tragic scene of desolation after the Clydebank blitz in 1941.

official – was that, within hours of landing, a message from the Renfrewshire County Constabulary was sent to Buchanan Street, through the Herald's Paisley correspondent, asking that all the biographical material in the files about Rudolf Hess be provided. The package included photographs, and such invaluable details as a description of certain distinguishing scars which Hitler's deputy had on his head, including the mark left by a beer mug thrown at him during a Nazi party rough-house in Munich. The Herald also saw to it that the package was delivered personally by an experienced member of the editorial staff.

The only claim the Herald made to a scoop – and that also the only valid one – was hinted in this sentence which was added when the story was officially released: 'Biographical records from the Glasgow Herald assisted detectives to identify Hess.'

Censorship was a continuing bugbear, partly because the censors, at least on the immediately local levels, were an excessively cautious crew, and it was not always easy to see the sense in their excisions. Robieson had a larger vision, and though faultless on important security, was happy to help the occasional small and harmless fish to slip through the net. We are indebted to James Shaw Grant, who was then the Editor of the Stornoway Gazette for reminding us of one of our minor evasions, by which it was contrived to report the loss of the SS Politician off Eriskay, with its cargo of whisky galore. A short paragraph in 'An Editorial Diary' announced simply that: 'Recent events in the Hebrides are regarded by the natives as the fulfilment of the poet's promise . . . "The spirits of our fathers shall rise from every wave".'

There were other restraints that the paper had to thole and understand, the one most nearly brought home to the paper being the bombing and destruction of Clydebank.

In war, inevitably, the Glasgow Herald went down in size, but not in circulation, thanks largely to the professional efficiency of an editor who so disposed his depleted resources of staff and space as to preserve the image, the news and the authority of its opinion. Some elderly but downy and skeely old hands were co-opted temporarily to fill the places of the younger members of Robieson's staff as they gradually vanished into the services. Of these, two noteworthy examples were A.W. Tilby and S.K. Radcliffe – the only trouble about Radcliffe being that while his mind was as keen and his critical pen was as sharp as a needle, his legs were not very reliable; so that his colleagues held their breath every time he started to make his way down the central staircase, for he was so irascible and independent that none would dare to insinuate a supporting hand under his elbow. Tilby, who was the intimate of the same political generation as Robert Bruce, and was the author of a definitive British Colonial History, remained with the paper until 1947, and died in harness.

Although Glasgow suffered only briefly from the bombers, it had its regular share of red warnings, and a topical use was found for the topmost storey of Rennie Mackintosh's water tower in Mitchell Street. This attic, which had also seen early service as a carrier-pigeon loft, was converted to a fire-watching outpost.

So far as anyone knew, no grave or unexplained incidents occurred up there during the five years of the emergency. But now we may have our doubts, for 35 years later, while Murray Ritchie was researching for one of the anniversary numbers, he made his way up the dark vertical ladder, past the water tower, to see where we had once stood watch for the enemy. He came back shaken, rather, one imagines, like the men who salvaged the drifting and unmanned Mary Celeste and found a half-eaten meal on the cabin table. In the pigeon loft the telephone was still there; but the receiver was off the hook, lying on the shelf, smothered in pigeon droppings.

There is in some quarters a popular slander that during the war the Glasgow Herald process department developed some secret skill in making facsimiles of Bank of England £5 notes. This is a malicious lie. All that happened was that, simply in the interest of the advancement of science, a few modest experiments were carried out with clothing coupons.

chapter 15

POST-WAR REFRESHMENT

WILLIAM ROBIESON was a scholarly and balancing influence upon those who wrote under his direction. Prejudice and passion tended to grow hazy round the edges after his briefings, and his sagacious authority had its effect over some unlikely subjects. During the first years of his regime, the Assistant Editor and chief leader-writer was J.M. Reid, an intransigent Scottish Nationalist. Yet even he tempered his pen on this subject. He did not, in fact, shuck off the curb and bolt until, toward the end of the war and on the death of William Heddle, he succeeded to the editorship of the Bulletin, which previously uncontentious picture paper – a high favourite and still a much missed staple of the older housewifery of Glasgow – he thereafter dedicated to this cause.

Though always cool towards militant Scottish Nationalism, the Herald regarded it without heat, and not infrequently with pleasantry. When Reid went, his place was taken by R.N. Biles, of Hampshire extraction, the former Literary

Editor, and in 1950 he was much more inclined than was the Editor to wax censorious about the theft of the Stone of Destiny. Robieson received the news with amusement, but decided, all things considered, that the appropriate editorial line should be to disapprove.

There was a diverting foray along the cultural furrows in this field in the first year after the war, which was a time of reawakening enthusiasms, when James Fergusson, a future Keeper of the Records of Scotland, but then a leader-writer, reviewing a couple of books of Lallans poetry on the Scottish Home Service, described Hugh Mac-Diarmid's 'synthetic Scots' as affected and horrible jargon howked out of dictionaries, and re-christened it Plastic Scots 'because any fragment or gobbet of language can be flung into it, and the result can be punched into whatever shape you like'. The Editorial Diary, then anonymous, but not written by Fergusson, took up the theme with a short lesson on how to compose in this medium.

There followed an at once comic and dreadfully pontifical correspondence that lasted three weeks, and involved most of the practitioners of Lallans, including Hugh MacDiarmid, and most learnedly, Douglas Young, the Greek scholar and the composer of what he himself called 'antran blads'. There were thirty published letters, with the 'Diary' intruding now and again when the pot seemed to need stirring; it might have gone on longer had a whisper not arrived that one of the protagonists had taken such offence at a disrespectful comment in one of the editorial squibs that he was contemplating legal action. So the rarified but funny logomachy was wound up with the very nearly Shakespearian quotation: 'The rest is dumbdeid.'

And so as supplies increased and the staff began turning up again in their demob suits, the paper passed discreetly into a more spacious and optimistic time, which was best demonstrated in the Edinburgh Festival, and the exuberance, not to say the unstinted columns, with which the Herald covered the music, the drama, the pictures, and the opening ceremonies and pageants which all, or nearly all, the Provosts in Scotland attended in the ermine and crimson that the Lord Lyon, crying in the wilderness, told them they had no entitlement to. It was such an expansive time for the descriptive writers, what with Indian independence, and Everest and the Coronation, that it is only with an effort of memory that one recalls it also included Korea.

Key figures who joined the staff in the war remained; like Tilby; and Colin Milne who came over from the Citizen and who, when I returned from a four year sabbatical in the RAF to reclaim the space at the bottom of the leader-page, became Literary Editor and theatre critic, and decorated these positions for ten years with distinction from his encyclopaedic acquaintance with famous plays and players from long before until long after Forbes Robertson.

Then there was, too, the youthful and vigorous intake of self-confident opinion-expressers: Alastair Hetherington, who left the Herald to go to, and subsequently mastermind, the Guardian: and at least one other who was to be, even then, both seen and heard. When the corridors echoed with swearing, noisy imprecations, and a good deal of loud advice, the staff knew that Alastair Burnet, now the very exemplar of composure on ITV, was in the television room watching cricket.

Nor should we forget that there was at this time at least one intrepid ambassador who, nationally and professionally, was ardent to keep the paper's end up against what might fairly be described as fearful odds. As uncompromising in his literary style, as he was jealous in honour, the then Football Correspondent sent this footnote from Basle to his report of the 1955 World Cup match between Uruguay and England:

> We in Scotland should thank our stars, with only small Celtic and Rangers minorities to disturb our game from the terracing. I can write of the conduct of the Uruguayan followers with especial authority, for at the end of yesterday's gruelling contest, one of them joined with the Uruguayan rabble who passed for press-men, and deliberately smashed a bottle on the press table almost under my nose.
>
> As a Scotsman, I am proud to say that the necessary punitive measures were immediately taken, whereupon the exuberant one emulated most of his heroes of the playing field and grovelled like a whipped cur.

We were later assured that the Swiss police, when they took a hand, agreed handsomely that the blow was well and fairly struck.

Sir William, who was knighted in 1948, had been made an LL.D. of Glasgow University in 1943. His interests and his preferred contacts outside the Glasgow Herald were substantially academic. He was Chancellor's Assessor to the Glasgow University Court. His other unflagging interest and loyalty was to the 6th Cameron Highlanders, an exclusively First World War unit that had been recruited largely from the mining districts of Lanarkshire and from the cloisters of Glasgow University. Indeed, their tribal song was 'Ygorra'. The 6th Camerons were disbanded in 1918, and never re-embodied. But the survivors, a striking cross-section of their catchment area, met annually to dine and refight old battles; a diminishing company that faded away only in 1977, when Sir William, one of the last half dozen of them, along with General Sir Philip Cristison (who on these occasions was addressed only as 'Lieutenant') wound up the little comradely society, and sent their trophy to the Regimental Museum at Fortrose.

Sir William retired in 1955, when he travelled frequently in Italy. He was the twelfth Editor of the Glasgow Herald, and by any standard, human, intellectual or professional, he was far from being the least of these. He died in 1977.

'Hello Happiness' was the title of a photographic competition organised from Manchester. Herald photographer Ian Hossack won the £1000 first prize with this picture of a disabled table tennis player at a sports meeting in Glasgow.

Eric Liddell winning the 400 metres at the Olympic Games in 1924 — an event to be commemorated nearly sixty years later with the film 'Chariots of Fire'. His style contrasts vividly with that of the modern runner, Alan Wells, Scotland's 100-metre Olympic gold medallist in 1980 — one of the photographs in the portfolio which won Arthur Kinloch the title Photographer of the Year.

The tackle in an Old Firm match in 1931 that lives on in Scottish football memories . . . Johnny Thompson, the Celtic keeper, dives towards the advancing Sam English. Thompson died from head injuries; English was broken in spirit for the rest of his life.

One of the great moments in Scottish rugby . . . Billy Steele, with David Duckham hanging on, scores Scotland's fourth try in the 1971 centenary match between Scotland and England at Murrayfield. Scotland won 26-6.

Football starts at an early age in Glasgow – even if the 'tanner ba'' sometimes gives way to soft drink cans. Practice when young can lead to skills like those of Alan Morton of Rangers – the 'Wee Blue Devil'.

Scotland's Olympic gold medallist, David Wilkie, as swimmers know him, and on a more formal occasion after receiving the insignia of his MBE award.

Kings of the ring – Benny Lynch and Jim Watt, who brought world boxing titles to Scotland.

A triumphant moment for Scottish football. Billy McNeill holds aloft the European Cup after Celtic beat Inter-Milan 2-1 at Lisbon in 1967, and became the first British club to win the championship.

Some pictures tell their own story – as when Jock Stein relinquished the managership of Celtic after 14 years to become a director. Billy McNeill, the new manager appointed in June 1978, is shaking hands with chairman Desmond White.

Between 1962 and 1973 Scottish drivers Jim Clark and Jackie Stewart dominated world championship Grand Prix racing with 25 and 27 title race wins apiece. Clark, a Duns farmer who died in a formula two race in West Germany in 1968, won the championship in 1963 and 1965, while Stewart, from Dumbuck, Dunbartonshire, scored his record number of wins with titles in 1969, 1971 and 1973. Clark was one of the greatest natural talents of all time, while Stewart brought a new level of professionalism and entrepreneurial skills to the sport.

THE MAN WHO LUNCHED WITH HITLER

AT THE TIME of writing, James Holburn, hale and hearty in his early 80's, is back in Alyth, where he went to school when his father was the local Church of Scotland minister. He is the widest travelled of all the Herald's editors. He has been on speaking terms with more heads of states than all his predecessors and successors put together. As Editor of the Glasgow Herald for the last ten years of his active newspaper career, he put by-lines in the paper, put news on the front page and put women into senior positions in the editorial department – remember Dr Wallace's laughable prophecy in 1906. It was as a Times correspondent that he did his globe-trotting for the better part of twenty years, but it was on the sub-editors' desk of the Herald that he cut his professional teeth.

The most sinister of his acquaintances on the international beat was, of course, Adolf Hitler, with whom he lunched at Nuremberg in 1938 at the time of a party rally. And his immediate table companions at that repast were Hess and

Ribbentrop. He spent several years in Germany for The Times, and in a temporary detachment from that office, he was accredited to the Nationalist forces in the Spanish Civil War, and was near enough to Guernica to make an eye-witness report that does not totally agree with what has become the received history of the incident.

From Germany, just before the outbreak of war, he went to Moscow, to spend some frustrating years producing despatches which seldom passed the censor. While he was never allowed to meet Stalin, he knew Molotov well, but not well enough to swell the tide of reliable news between Moscow and London. After further assignments as a war-correspondent in Africa and the Middle East, he went to Turkey and thence to India. The war was still on, but independence was in the offing, and he made close and critical contact with the protagonists. Of Nehru, whom he knew well enough, he had no good opinion; but with Jinnah, whom he knew much better, he found a considerable affinity; and professionally this was a fruitful time, for he enjoyed also the confidence of the two Viceroys, the Marquess of Linlithgow and Lord Wavell, who had gone there as C-in-C in 1941, and became Viceroy and Governor-General in 1943. After the war, he was Times correspondent and by 1955, when Sir William Robieson went looking for his old Buchanan Street colleague with the editorship of the Glasgow Herald in his gift, James Holburn was diplomatic correspondent in London.

The tempo of the new regime was energetic from the start. Perhaps the paper had become a little set in its ways, and surprisingly enough in a trade in which personal vanity is never far absent, there was some initial misgiving when the Editor made it known that features, special articles, and major news stories would carry the name of their author. There had no doubt been certain potential advantages in being unidentified in the days when the paper, itself a personified entity using the editorial 'We', took all the responsibility for what was printed. There was a quick recovery from that fleeting modesty.

There was equal, and better founded misgiving when on the morning of 6 October 1958, the Glasgow Herald, for the first time in 107 years, appeared with news on the front page. Till then it had been taken for granted that the first thing Glasgow wanted to read in the morning was the Births, Deaths and Marriages (the Hatches, Matches and Dispatches). But that tradition, too, faded without a whimper.

And what was the front page news that day? The three-column lead on the left was a report on 'More Terrorism in Cyprus'; followed by the suspension of the Chinese bombardment of an island between Taiwan and the mainland; and to round off, a double column of 'Explosions in Tennessee', that had to do with the school race-riots. On the other side of the page, there was the more progressive news 'Daily Comet Flights by December', with a picture. Readers also learned, single-column top, that Duncan Sandys had returned from defence talks in America.

Of local causes célèbres during this period, the most sensational, the longest drawn out, and the most exhaustively reported was the trial

and execution of the mass murderer, Peter Thomas Anthony Manuel.
And, of course, further afield, there was Suez, where the paper had
the advantage of the Editor's special knowledge of the area and its
passions.

One of the more eye-catching Holburn innovations was the creation
for the first time of an exclusive features department. As well as the
production of supplements for special occasions, the conduct of the
Week-End Page, and the placing and supervision of special articles,
this department had responsibility for the Trade Review, a publication
which merits a particular note; because it has been the outstanding
example of the newspaper's commercial importance.

The Glasgow Herald Trade Review began in 1901 as an eight-page supplement about engineering and shipbuilding. By 1907 it was an annual magazine in its own right, with its interests extending to textiles and other industries. It analysed the state of trade by areas from central Scotland to northern England. In continued to grow in size and influence until, some 25 years ago, C.A. Oakley wrote: 'It has become one of the foremost reviews circulating throughout the world.' Its major importance rested in its survey of shipping, specifically launched tonnage. And some measure of that international importance can be seen from an approach that was made during the Holburn years. The Trade Review was then of such size that it was printed in sections over a period of some weeks. So anxious were the Japanese that their shipping construction figure should be exactly up to date that they sent a delegation to Glasgow to persuade the Herald to reprint, if necessary at their expense, a 'sig', already in type, containing a statistical table which the Japanese had themselves provided that did not include a reference to some launches which had taken place during the immediately previous month.

When things went wrong with the Herald – as they regularly do in any paper – Robieson was seldom reproachful with the sinners, being more inclined to take the blame himself, saying: 'I should have noticed that on the proofs'. Holburn was not so gentle, somewhat to the discomfiture of a small leavening of editorial prima donnas who had blossomed in the earlier regime. This was a good and salutary discipline, for he knew exactly what he was about; and by a fairly regular printed programme of circulated anonymous blame and named praise, he tightened up the syntax, and the headlines, and the creative subediting of the paper. Of course, he had his own prejudices and areas of incomplete enlightenment, which the staff tolerated without too much resentment. The personal incident which I have in mind was when he summoned the Editorial Diarist (as the writer of the daily space at the bottom of the leader page was then called) to chide me for my too frequent references to the American Wild West, and to such characters as the one he referred to as 'Big Bob Hitchcock'. (For the deprived minority who may be unfamiliar with these arcana, he meant Wild Bill Hickok.)

James Holburn also experienced, without particularly enjoying, the intrusion of a team of management consultants (at, we believe, very considerable expense), who lived with us for six months without discovering any inefficiency in his method of running the editorial department.

A fine action shot of the Duke of
Edinburgh driving at Scone Palace,
Perth, in 1979.

Opposite, top.
'She spoke to me!' Duncan Dingsdale's
award-winning picture shows the
delight of a Cub on being presented to
the Queen during a visit to Hawick.
Right, Duncan catches the Queen in
not quite such a pleasant conversation
with a horse.

Opposite.
This picture by James Thomson of
Princess Anne accepting a jelly baby,
won him £1000. Colleague Ian Hossack
won another award with a picture of
Prince Charles squeezing into a go-kart
made by pupils at All Saints' School,
Barmulloch, Glasgow.

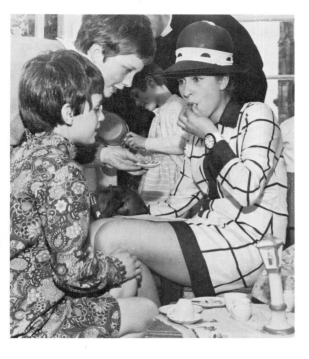

chapter 17

THE TAKE-OVER BATTLE

The late Lord Fraser –
father of Sir Hugh

THE GLASGOW HERALD'S most traumatic and, depending on whether your point of view is editorial or mercantile, the most exciting period in its long history of survival, occurred during 52 days in the autumn of 1964. The famous, if indeed it may not now be described as the notorious, take-over battle for the control of Outram, was waged between Hugh Fraser and Roy Thomson from 2 September to 24 October. It was a devious and ruthless battle of share buying, and competitive bidding, with 51 per cent of the capital as the winning target. The operation was hedged with misdirection and secrecy; the occasion is unique because the tactics and strategies that won the engagement for Hugh Fraser are no longer allowed.

The historic essence of the case is that Fraser (using SUITs as his main vehicle) made only two offers to the shareholders, while Thomson made five; and that in the end Fraser got his control for nearly £1,000,000 less than Thomson's last cash offer. The exact figures are: Thomson's fifth and last bid (October 17) 31s 7½d in cash for each Outram share, valuing the Company at £8,294,383; as against Scottish & Universal Investments offer of one SUITs' 5s ordinary share, plus 6s 6d cash for each Outram share. This offer, posted on October 15 and made unconditional, valued the company at £7,343,644; a difference of some £950,000.

How this came about is a story as complex and as fascinating as a fictional financial thriller. And not all of those who watched it from the sidelines found it a pretty sight. The financial considerations on both sides were decorated, while not obscured, by promises and appeals to local sentiment, a competition, this, in which Hugh Fraser enjoyed, and made effective use of, a distinct advantage. Fraser's financial and tactical adviser throughout was John B. Kinross, a highly charged and experienced company negotiator. He kept a daily record of the affair, to every detail of which he was privy; and six years after the event, he wrote a full and candid account of the forays, the manoeuvres, the campaign conferences, and the misinformations which combined to make what is conceded to be a famous victory. He did this at the request of the Department of Economic History at Glasgow University. It is upon him that we rely for the detail of most of what follows.

Thomson had for long had an acquisitive eye on the Glasgow Herald, but his tentative approaches had stirred no favourable response. Then he fired his first salvo with a letter, delivered by hand on 2 September 1964, to the Directors of George Outram and Company Limited, from the Thomson Organisation, London. It was an offer, made without any preliminary courtesies, for the share capital of Outram.

Lord Thomson of Fleet

The letter went on, 'Urgent steps are necessary to strengthen the national Press of Scotland, in particular, the "quality" newspapers. The Directors of Thomson Organisation further believe that the provision of first-class newspaper services and coverage in Scotland can best be achieved by aggressive development of these quality newspapers rather than by expansion of Scottish editions of English newspapers. For these reasons, the Directors of Thomson have decided to seek a strong link between Outram and Scotsman Publications Ltd, through a Scottish holding company, directed and managed from Scotland. The Board of Scottish Thomson Organisation will consist predominantly of residents. . . . It is the intention to continue Outram as a separate organisation . . . and to preserve the separate identities of the Glasgow Herald and the Scotsman.' The offer was to acquire all the 5,245,460 ordinary shares of 5s each of Outram, for 20s each.

The response of the Outram Board (of which Hugh Fraser was then deputy Chairman, he having come into the firm in 1959) was to make an immediate announcement to the Scottish Stock Exchange advising shareholders not to sell their holdings.

The next day, Sir Hugh was appointed Chairman, as the best man to deal with impending crisis, 'for he possessed a wealth of experience of take-over battles'. Then came the first of the press statements that were to keep the pot boiling for the better part of two months.

'In my considered opinion,' said Fraser, 'it would be contrary to the best interests of Scotland and a serious loss if the Glasgow Herald and all the Scottish art and tradition it offers and represents were to be removed from Scotland. . . . I see the present situation as a challenge to Scottish enterprise and resource. . . . I shall use every endeavour to see that the control of George Outram shall remain in Scottish hands.' A message to all shareholders recommended rejection of the Thomson offer.

It was at this point, when experienced field commanders were needed for the campaign, that John Kinross was called in, and from then on the contact was constant through each 24 hours.

'The first few weeks,' says Kinross, 'were spent in sparring by both sides. Thomson tried hard to gain the support of the Outram Board, and Sir Hugh was approached by several emissaries who argued that without a union with the Scotsman, the Glasgow Herald was doomed. Sir Hugh was offered the chairmanship of the combined company, but all these discussions broke down when the Thomson people insisted that (purely for purposes of consolidating the profits) they must have 50% plus one vote.' Kinross warned that what was coming was total war, and that the only answer was outright possession of Outram shares. And so Sir Hugh started to buy the shares whenever they were offered.

The question of a counter bid now loomed, and it was decided that SUITs would be the instrument for this. SUITs, Hugh Fraser personally, the Outram Board and the House of Fraser between them at this point held 10.65% of the Outram capital; the Thomson companies held none, but 'this was only a modest handicap in our favour'.

On 2 October Thomson made its second, and higher bid with 'an ingenious attempt to break down the opposition on grounds of Scottish Nationalism'. The new offer was one 5s ordinary share in Thomson Scottish Organisation, plus 3s cash, with the guarantee that (should the offer succeed and Thomson Scottish qualify for quotation on the Stock Exchange) that the profits would be not less that £1.35 million per annum for three years. This, on face value, boosted the offer to £6,032,275.

Bids three, four and five which followed were variants upon this, with additional promises directed towards national sentiment. For example, the Thomson Board would be enlarged to include representatives from both east and west of Scotland; Outram would be a separate organisation with its own west of Scotland Board.

In the meantime, the Fraser team was in continuous session, and the SUITs' counter offer having been agreed, it was decided that Fraser should resign from the Outram Board, so that he might have a free hand to continue a fight in which no holds would be barred. The offer was 9 SUITs for every 8 Outram shares, or 23s 6d cash, which made the bid worth £6,163,415.

With the offer there went out a public appeal to sentiment. Thus, Sir

Hugh: 'The proposal to enlarge the Scottish representation on the Board of Thomson Scottish Organisation might at first sight appear to be attractive, but it is of little importance when compared with the hard fact of where the control of the company resides (London). With these thoughts uppermost in my mind, I am not prepared to stand idly by and take the risk of seeing the independence of the Glasgow Herald lost by default. . . . This is precisely the threat posed by the Thomson Organisation, a threat which clearly will continue to be with us unless it is disposed of once and for all. . . . It has never been my desire or intention to acquire control of Outrams, either directly or indirectly, but in the situation which has now developed, I have reached the conclusion that I have no other course left open to me.'

That just about ended the jockeying for position. Now the undercover operations began, with their attendant devices of smoke screens, counter claims and infiltrations. Since he was the agent in the field, who better than John Kinross to tell what he did and how he did it?

'That Monday (5 October) for the first time, I started to operate in the market, buying both Outram and SUITs' shares in Scotland and London. . . . I also spent some time building up a short list of Scottish brokers who we believed all had a worthwhile number of clients holding Outram shares. From this list I withdrew the names of the Glasgow and Edinburgh brokers who, I ascertained, were in touch with Thomson. I kept in close touch with the others, and a few days later, I had installed on my desk in London, a new direct telephone, the number of which was known only to these firms. If any of these brokers received a selling order in Outrams, I invited them to telephone me at this number and deal direct with me at the middle market price. In this way, they got a slightly better price for their client, we got the shares, and the market was unaware of any transaction. I had lunch in my room each day, and seldom left my three telephones. It worked very well, and by the end it proved to be a considerable factor in deciding the outcome of the battle. . . I destroyed all details of Outram dealings each day for reasons of security.'

The interest of the rest of the national press was voracious. Not a day passed without apparently expert analysis and evaluation. While most of the papers remained more or less impartial and factual, there were two that took sides – or at least two city editors. Frederick Ellis of the Daily Express was a Fraser man, who in effect joined the team 'and fed us with all the current information as it reached Fleet Street'. Patrick Sergeant of the Daily Mail, while less well-disposed, himself innocently contributed to the ultimate Thomson defeat. It was all this business of the race to buy up the crucial number of shares.

On Monday 12 October Sergeant interviewed Kinross, and asked him directly what percentage of Outram capital he now held. Kinross replied that, of course, that was obviously something he could not discuss: to which Sergeant replied: 'Perhaps it isn't necessary. I have good reason to believe you now have around 30%.'

Again, let Kinross take it from there: 'I have – unfortunately – always blushed too easily when embarrassed and, at that moment, I certainly felt so. The figure, the holy of holies, was known only to Sir Hugh, myself and two or three other people. At that moment, the true figure was fully 40%, but the question was so near the bone that I felt my colour rising. Sergeant saw it too, and drew the understandable conclusion that he had scored a bull's eye. He smiled broadly and got up to go. Realising what was happening, I said nothing, and indeed stopped trying to control my face – it had suddenly become an asset in those few seconds.'

The following day, the Daily Mail reported authoritatively that Sir Hugh Fraser had accumulated 30% of Outram. This had a lulling effect on the opposition and the team went on with its task of getting the maximum number of Outram shares in the minimum of time.

On 12 October Thomson made his fourth bid, with an increased cash offer of 28s 1½d per share. This was followed by SUITs' second and last bid, the terms of which were one SUITs' ordinary share for each Outram share, plus 6s 6d in cash, making it worth £7,343,644. By this time, the Fraser colleagues had 43% of the Outram shares, and although still short of the essential 51%, they had sufficient confidence in the promises of Scottish backers and shareholders, as to take the risk of 'going unconditional'.

In the case of Outram, had no more acceptances been received after the bid was declared unconditional, SUITs would have been left with a minority holding, and unable to withdraw. This declaration was made on 16 October; and the next day Thomson announced his fifth offer, which added 3s 6d in cash for each Outram share. This made the bid £8,294,383 compared with SUITs' £7,343,644.

But by the time it was announced, Fraser already had nearly 50%, lacking only two local holdings which, without too much strain, he bought – or had bought for him – during a pause in a golf game on the outskirts of Glasgow. Thomson, unaware of this final coup, continued to buy, expensively, in the market. And on Monday 19 October Sir Hugh stated to the press: 'From the information available to me I am confident that the total number of shares committed to, or owned by SUITs, exceeds 50% of the capital of Outram.'

Roy Thomson did not believe him, and issued his own statement that: 'The Directors of Thomson Scottish attach no importance to vague and unconfirmed statements to the effect that Scottish and Universal Trust has "assurances" of "support" from certain institutional holders. It would be unusual for responsible boards of directors of institutions to commit themselves so far in advance of the closing date of either offer . . . the Thomson offer is clearly and considerably superior to the Fraser offer . . . and the shareholders cannot fail to recognise this.'

The official announcement of the Fraser victory was made in the Merchants Hall in Glasgow during the SUITs' annual general meeting on Friday 23 October. The loser, not a little surly, on being asked to comment, replied: 'All I can say is that if Sir Hugh Fraser has won, the shareholders of Outram and Scotland itself will quite certainly have lost.'

And the decisive factor? 'The meticulous care with which we organised our buying of Outram shares . . . and the success we achieved in keeping the eventual scale of this absolutely confidential.'

Not everyone found the take-over battle edifying. As a running story it was stimulating and newsworthy, much in the same way as are natural disasters and the more personal sort of political conflicts. Here were two giants of their kind going for the throat. A General Election was in progress and the daily exchanges made nourishing fodder for the local candidates on both sides; although their vocal influence was really a bit of supererogation; for the local sentiment of the Outram shareholders was so committed that the dice were pretty heavily loaded against Thomson from the start. There was a general feeling that he already had too many newspapers; a sentiment, that, most defiantly expressed by the Inverness Courier (the tiniest enclave of independence sitting in the middle of his Highland empire). The aged Editor and owner declared that his little journal would never be taken over, even if Roy Thomson did own 136 newspapers, 23 of them in Scotland. The British Weekly said that it was the Glasgow Herald that should be taking over the Scotsman. The Labour candidates, a little more vociferously than the Tories, condemned the whole operation as 'big business at its worst'. And The Times, whose own troubles were still to come, observed the machinations and the moves with a certain superior detachment, conceding that Thomson might be a beneficent force in the newspaper world; but adding: 'Even if he were the Archangel Gabriel, we would also believe that he has quite enough papers in the United Kingdom already. *A fortiori* it cannot be right that so long as there are two leading papers in Scotland they should be in the same hands.'

As for James Holburn, the Editor of the Glasgow Herald, he was, at least theoretically, a little less ill-disposed than some (or indeed many) towards Roy Thomson, whom he recognised professionally as a newspaper man of sorts; but he was of a mind to call down a plague on both their houses. Although himself a member of the Board of Outram, he remained a disapproving onlooker for most of that time, entering the lists only once at the height of the struggle to write an uncompromising leading article in which he deplored the unseemly spectacle of a great newspaper being haggled over in the market place 'like a beast in the cattle ring'. His impartial distaste for the Fraser-Thomson duel had not particularly endeared him to the new administration, and his retirement at the age limit four months later (at the end of February 1965) was not delayed, although Lord Fraser (elevated to the peerage in December 1964) had not yet finally decided who should succeed him.

George Macdonald Fraser – author

George Macdonald Fraser, his deputy of a few months' standing was appointed acting Editor and ran the paper with imagination and efficiency for several months, until A.K. Warren, the City Editor, and one of Hugh Fraser's most steadfast staff lieutenants during the confrontation of the two master manipulators, was appointed to the office.

Then George Fraser, reverting to the duties of deputy, found spare time in the midnight hours to return to a manuscript which he had begun some years before while convalescing from a broken arm. He finished 'Flashman', an instant and now long multiplied success which, for publishing reasons which need not be detailed here, deprived the Herald of his services at almost a moment's notice and sent him into productive exile in the Isle of Man.

FROM STAGE COACH TO SPACE MODULE

ON 6 NOVEMBER 1964 (the original closing date) SUITs had acquired 81.8 per cent of the Outram shares. By 9 December the holding was 88.2 per cent, just short of the 90 per cent necessary to allow the compulsory purchase of the balance. And there the transactions lingered for four-and-a-half years, for there was still a decisive nucleus of stubborn local shareholders, reluctant to part with their interest in such a reliable and old-established good thing as the Glasgow Herald and its thriving brood.

In April 1969 SUITs bought Thomson's holding of 535,009 shares; and in December of that year acquired those remaining Outram shares which brought their holding above the required 90 per cent. This was a consummation which Hugh Fraser did not live to see. He was elevated to the peerage as Baron Fraser of Allander some two months after his victory over Roy Thomson. On 6 November 1966 at the age of 63 he suffered a fatal heart attack, and was succeeded in his chairmanship of the company by his son, Hugh,

Alastair Warren

who renounced the peerage. We thus come to the end of the communal, wide and fragmented ownership of the Glasgow Herald, Outram having become a wholly owned subsidiary, albeit an important one, of Scottish and Universal Investments.

It was into this new environment of administrative and technical readjustment that Alastair Warren was projected. New printing practices were in prospect; and although it was yet to be some considerable time before the computer took over from hot metal, a system of typesetting on tape was already being introduced. Management, too, entered more visibly and continuously upon the editorial floor.

Alastair Warren came with the best of local connections. He is a member of a long established business and engineering Glasgow family; and his professional qualifications were in economics and commerce. He made the transition from City Editor to Editor unobtrusively, and without the occasional abrasiveness of his predecessor. The immediate noticeable effect was an informality in the day-to-day running of his department. In this relaxed approach he was, in fact, the first of the editors who was addressed by his first name by all but the most junior members of his team. He showed himself to be a ready leader-writer and a valuable familiar of the business community both here and in the south. And he contributed freely to the other parts of the paper, even to the extent of nodding to an earlier editorial tradition of contributing a modest amount of verse which found its way into the Week-end Pages.

The most climactic occurrence of his editorship was the Moon landing of the early hours of 21 July 1969. That may indeed have been a great step for mankind, but it was an anxiously delayed one for the small congregation assembled round the television set in the Editor's room. Edition time was already arrived. The module had touched down. The historic eight-column front page heading was in type, with the second heading anticipating the first step upon the surface there below it. The stereo plates were already locked into the printing presses. The start button was just waiting to be pressed; but Neil Armstrong was being unconscionably slow about coming down the ladder. Until he set foot on the Moon, the operation was not safely accomplished. The chief sub-editor had the incongruously attentive but far-away look of the man who was mulling over the possibility of a more depressing headline and opening paragraph. The caseroom overseer was calculating how quickly he might be able to do the resetting; the head of the stereo department was making his own assessment; and the machine room manager was looking turn about at the television screen and the clock on the wall, saying: 'Look, I can't give you more than another five minutes, or we'll never get the edition out in time.'

All the while, there were Armstrong's great thick space boots still on the third-top rung of the ladder – and staying there. The moment of

Man lands on the moon.

The Herald's first edition of Monday, 21 July 1969 – a giant step for mankind, but a nerve-racking night for journalists as well as US astronauts.

decision came when the man from the machine room with a last look at the clock, stood up and said: 'That's it, then. What are you going to do?'

With the astronaut still six feet up in space, and not moving, it fell to my own decision to give the word: 'Let her run. But not a single copy of the paper must leave the place until you get the all-clear from this phone.'

We need not have worried. The presses were just beginning to pick up speed when Armstrong (clearly deciding that he had teased us long enough) continued and completed his descent, and left us with what may or may not have been the illusion that we were the first on the streets with the news. And that was the Glasgow Herald safely into the Space Age.

Summer's always a time
when photographers are
sent out to find
topical pictures.
Different weather
brings different results.

Housing is
Glasgow's oldest problem,
and one which is
no nearer a solution now
than it was a century ago.
Opposite page –
the dereliction that still
surrounds some tenements.
Right –
the determination and pride
that still kept a pensioner
using her old range,
even in the 'Seventies.

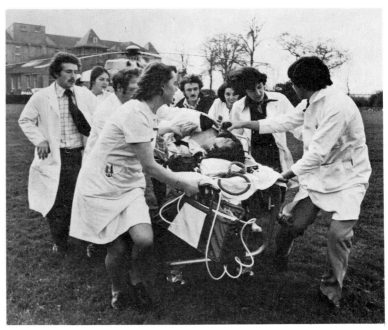

Glasgow's incomparable medical and nursing skills in action.
A heart attack victim arriving by helicopter
at the Southern General hospital
(award-winning picture by Stuart Patterson);
aiding victims at the Clarkston gas explosion disaster in 1971.

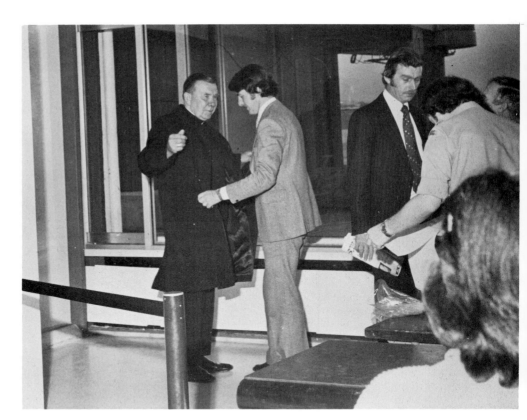

An unlikely suspect – but Cardinal Gray is still frisked by a security man at Turnhouse Airport. It won an award for Edinburgh chief photographer James Thomson in 1978.

Even serious situations can have their lighter side – the Army takes over in Edinburgh during the firemen's strike of 1977.

Two historic moments during Pope John Paul's visit to Scotland in 1982 – kissing Scottish soil on his arrival at Edinburgh; and passing beneath the statue of John Knox during his meeting with the Moderator of the General Assembly of the Church of Scotland, the Rt Reverend Professor John McIntyre.

A night shot by Edward Jones of the
QE2 in its fitting out basin at John
Brown's yard.

The Glasgow Herald was the only Scottish paper
to have its own reporter with the Task Force in the Falklands conflict.
Defence Correspondent Ian Bruce is pictured by the fox-hole
in which he was bombed and straffed by Argentine planes at Ajax Bay.
He witnessed the blowing up of HMS Antelope (below),
and was one of only two journalists
to accompany 45 Commando on the hazardous,
storm-swept northern march to Port Stanley.
His dispatches were published by every Scottish daily newspaper
and regularly quoted by radio and television.

Appendix 1

1974–1983

In July 1974 Alastair Warren left the Glasgow Herald to become Senior Editor of the Borders set of country papers published by the new sister organisation, Scottish & Universal Newspapers Limited (SUN). After a short delay, during which day-to-day control was vested in the Deputy Editor James Munro, another editor was found in Iain Lindsay-Smith, a former pupil of the Glasgow High School, who came to the Herald from the Yorkshire Post.

Lindsay-Smith made radical alterations in the make-up of the Glasgow Herald, redesigning and modernising the appearance and enlarging the news and features content of the paper, before going back down south to become Executive Editor of the Observer. He also played the bag-pipes, even on occasion in the time-honoured Rennie Mackintosh Editor's room. Alan Jenkins, who had an active interest in the computer production of newspapers, succeeded him, and oversaw the most recent physical developments in the paper.

When the Scottish Daily Express gave up its Glasgow operation, and after the failure of the doomed Daily News with Robert Maxwell as godfather, Outram took over the Albion Street premises and began the conversion to the total computer technology. The operation cost £13,000,000, and was completed after long and complex negotiations with the craft unions.

In the meantime, in 1979, Scottish & Universal Investments, with its George Outram subsidiary, was incorporated in the Lonrho empire. And when on 19 July 1980, the final transfer was made to Albion Street, after 112 years in Buchanan Street, this was the return of the Glasgow Herald to its cradle within hailing distance of Glasgow Cross and the plainstanes of the Tobacco Barons who had been its earliest readers.

Alan Jenkins relinquished the editorship of the Glasgow Herald in 1981 when he was succeeded by Arnold Kemp from the Scotsman, a member of a distinguished literary and journalistic family – and with a close and valued family connection with the Glasgow Herald. His father, Robert Kemp, the noted Scottish playright and author, was for many years a contributor (in succession to George Blake) of a weekly column of comment, opinion and reminiscence, to the 'Editorial Diary'. This daily feature on the leader page, which ran for more than forty years, still survives in slightly altered form in the personal and multi-authored columns which now take its place.

Appendix 2

THE BUSINESS MEN

It is an engaging reflection upon the Glasgow Herald's inherent genius for survival that the founding fathers of the paper, who reigned for the first 53 years of its existence, were two men who had been unable to manage their own affairs.

John Mennons tried to be a coalmaster, and failed; Samuel Hunter had made less than nothing of the business he toyed with before he took on the Glasgow Herald. However, the fact that to begin with he knew as little about newspaper production as he did about calendering, made no difference in the long run. Like his predecessor, he was well advised by an unobtrusive man-of-business.

This good management indeed can be extended a further twenty years, for George Outram was no mercantile innovator, but owed his comfortable existence to the good sense that left the management of the partnership's affairs to others.

The paper was blessed with a succession of shrewd godfathers, using the epithet in its original and infinitely more kindly sense. The first of these was Benjamin Mathie, the lawyer and town clerk of Rutherglen. He was not to begin with actually involved in the trading, but acted as Mennons' legal adviser, though it may be doubted if his advice was listened to when the Editor sold up and took to coal-mining. Some four years before he took this final step Mennons gave a one-third share in the business to his son Thomas; and in 1802 disposed of the rest to Benjamin Mathie for £900.

When Hunter joined them as a partner, it is a fair guess that they gave him his head only in matters editorial. When Thomas Mennons died in 1804 this was also the last of any Mennons' interest in the newspaper. His share went to Dr William Dunlop, and the day-to-day management devolved upon Hunter and Mathie.

The next significant change at the top came towards the end of Hunter's day, by which time Alexander Morrison had assumed the role of legal adviser, and inaugurated what might be called the dynastic control of the concern. In this he had a skeely and far-sighted coadjutor in William Dun (he of the finances in his trouser pocket) who had been with the Herald since 1811, and was now cashier. Between them they acquired the Hunter and Mathie interests, appointed George Outram Editor, provided him with shares and drew up a contract of partnership. This provided for 14 shares of which Morrison held 7, Dun 5, and Outram 2. The capital was £2800.

Under Outram, the business affairs were run by Morrison and Dun, who at the same time laid those foundations for the future of their kin which remained dominant in the share list until 1920, when George Outram and Co. went public.

The nephews of Dun, a bachelor with two married sisters, entered the management with, and after him, while Alexander Morrison had two sons in the directorate. In the next generations the Outram interest also multiplied, and was made no easier to follow in the later register of partners by the fact that the widow of William Reid Outram (George's son) remarried twice.

James Pagan was himself a good business man, whose interest finally passed to his son-in-law, James Kennedy of Dounholm.

By this time, it may be remembered, Alexander Sinclair, the first of the 'Two Office Boys' earlier mentioned, was on his way up, and he was decisive in the movements and ventures that swelled the coffers and the prestige of the Herald in the last quarter of the century.

As for the other 'Office Boy', it is upon him that we rely for the detail of the financial history of the early and middle years of George Outram, and the consolidations and expansions of his own time. He put this down some 35 years ago in a privately printed record, when the burden of his remit was to explain the 'financial structure based on an initial investment by John Mennons of not more than two hundred pounds sterling. To this no "new money" has ever been added, all increment in the value of the assets or the partnership of the company having come from profits earned or held in reserve . . .'

When the sums were done in 1921, the multiplication showed that that £200 had become £300,000, a fifteen-hundredfold increase.

The many changes recorded from the day when William Dun and Alexander Morrison each owned one half of the share capital of the company may be difficult to follow, but Ewing summarises them by saying that, when the private limited company was formed in 1903, the representatives of these two families still held, between them, one-half of the share capital, the Dun and Waters interests holding 37½% and the Morrison interests 12½%.

The complete register was as follows:

	SHARES
James C. Dun Waters	25
Mrs. A.M. Sutthery	10
Trustees Mrs Grace E. Waters	5
J.C. Dun Waters and Mrs A.M. Sutthery	5
Adam Morrison's Trust	15
Miss Jane Macphail	10
Dr Robert Gourlay	5
James Pagan's Trust	5
Dr Stoddart's Trust	5
Alexander Sinclair	5
John Hartley Perks	5
John P.M'L. Watters	5
Dr George T.B. Watters	5
James Kennedy	5
James Outram and John D. Outram	5
Captain Stewart P. Falls	1
	120

(The unfamiliar names in this list are those of the inheritors-in-law of the early newspaper-adventurers.)

1920 and After

Ewing goes on to explain that when it was resolved to form a public company, a few months after the end of the First World War, the future was very uncertain. No one could have predicted the rapid trade recovery which then took place, and to this the early success achieved by the new company may, in part, be attributed. Full advantage of this recovery could not have been taken by a company crippled in its material or financial resources, and to the moderate valuation placed by the vendor company on the assets transferred, some at least of the success is due. How otherwise would it be possible to account for the fact that, in addition to paying dividends which over seven years averaged more than seventeen per cent., the company was able to redeem its debenture issue of £120,000 and purchase the Evening Citizen out of reserves, and yet increase its issued capital from £480,000 in 1920, to £876,222 at the end of 1926?

1920	Nominal Capital	£600,000	
	of which issued and fully paid		£480,000
1922	Purchase of the business of James Hedderwick & Sons, Ltd, printers and publishers of the Evening Citizen; the purchase price being paid partly in cash and partly by the issue of 6789 shares in George Outram & Company, Ltd, thus increasing its issued capital by		6,789
	to		£486,789
1923	Redemption of Debentures and issue of bonus shares in proportion of one share for each five shares		97,358
	bringing issued capital to		£584,147
1926	Issue of bonus shares in proportion of one share for two shares		282,075
	bringing issued capital at the end of 1926 to		£876,222
	Issued capital at end of 1926		£876,222
	To reconcile Capital with the amount at which it stands in 1948,		
1941	Repayment of capital, ten shillings per share		438,111
	Issued Capital converted into Stock and now held in 876,222 units of 10/-		£438,111
1948	Issued Capital		£438,111

THE BOARD OF DIRECTORS
The members of the Board in 1920 were:
James Gourlay (Chairman), Arthur Melbourne Sutthery, William Hay, Andrew Morrison Macgeorge, Henry Drummond Robertson, David McCowan, Laurence MacBrayne.

On the death of Mr Robertson on 27 December 1926, he was succeeded by James Davidson, who had been Editor of the Evening Times and of the Bulletin.

Mr Hay resigned in 1931 and died on 1 February 1947. He was succeeded by John Spencer Muirhead, D.S.O., M.C.

A.M. Sutthery retired in 1933 and was succeeded by A. McLean Ewing. Mr Sutthery died on 16 May 1937.

James Davidson died on 29 June 1937, and was succeeded by Col. Norman Kennedy, C.B.E., D.S.O.

Sir David McCowan died on 25 May 1937, and was succeeded by James Willock.

Laurence MacBrayne retired in April 1939, and was succeeded by Bryce B. Morrison. Mr MacBrayne died on 7 July 1941.

James Willock died on 13 May 1942, and was succeeded by Robert Gourlay.

In March 1948, James Gourlay, who had been Chairman of the company from its formation in 1920, resigned the Chairmanship, but agreed to continue as a Director. Alex. McLean Ewing was appointed to succeed him as Chairman.

The Board of Directors at March 1948:
Alex. McLean Ewing (Chairman), Andrew M. Macgeorge (Deputy Chairman), James Gourlay, John Spencer Muirhead, Norman Kennedy, Bryce B. Morrison, Robert Gourlay.

When, for personal reasons, Mr Ewing asked to be relieved from the Chairmanship, Mr Andrew Morrison Macgeorge was appointed to succeed him, with John Spencer Muirhead as Deputy Chairman.

The Board of Directors at December 1948:
Andrew Morrison Macgeorge (Chairman), John Spencer Muirhead (Deputy Chairman), James Gourlay, Alex. McLean Ewing, Norman Kennedy, Bryce B. Morrison, Robert Gourlay.

This, with the addition, and departure in their turn, of the editorial directors, Wm Adair, Sir Wm Robieson, and James Holburn, remained the Board of Directors until 1959, when Sir Hugh Fraser was invited to join.

On the retirement of Bryce B. Morrison, and of

the Company Secretary Thomas White, A.G. Stephen and Gordon B. Allan (both of whom later became members of the Board) were appointed General Manager and Company Secretary respectively.

When the take-over passed the control effectively into Hugh Fraser's own hand, the Board was reconstructed to include Esmond Wright (the historian), Daniel Fennell (a SUITs executive), Dr J. Wright (Hugh Fraser's personal physician), and Arthur Hill (an old and experienced business friend and the owner of a knitwear factory on the Borders), and Hugh Fraser junior, who became Chairman on the death of his father in 1965.

A.G. Stephen, who was appointed Managing Director in March 1965, died in November 1970. He was succeeded by W.K. Forgie, who had been brought into the SUITs group by Sir Hugh and was appointed an Outram director in April 1970. He resigned in November 1976.

In June 1979, SUITs was acquired by Lonrho and the present members of the board of George Outram are: D.K. Harris (Chairman), J.R. Crawford (Deputy Chairman/Acting Managing Director), T.F. Cassidy (Deputy Managing Director), K.A. Graham (Director), J.H. Fyfe (Director), I.J. Irvine (Financial Director), C.M. Wilson (Editorial Director).

John Crawford joined the advertisement department of George Outram & Co. in 1953, rising through successive posts to become General Manager of the Glasgow Herald and Evening Times in 1971, and Managing Director of the company in 1975. He is a director of SUITs and the Observer.

Ian Irvine was appointed Chief Accountnt to George Outram in 1965, and became Financial Director in 1975.

Hot metal in its heyday — below, a battery of linecasting machines in the old caseroom at Buchanan Street. Right, plates being cast in the foundry before being clamped to the rotary presses.

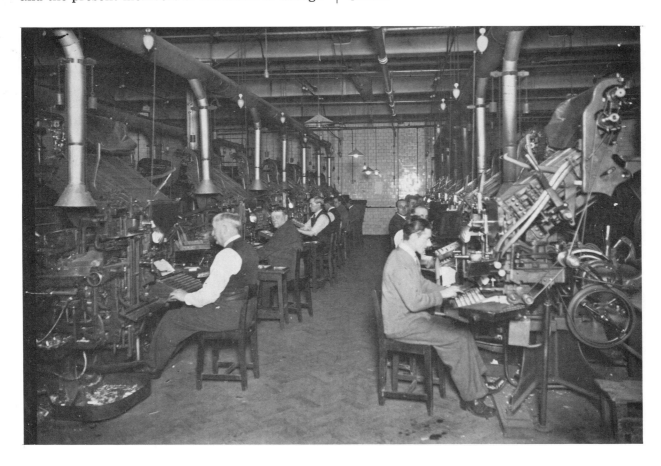

Appendix 3
INTO THE NEW TECHNOLOGY
by Murray Ritchie

The last issue of the Glasgow Herald to be printed by the traditional hot metal method appeared on Saturday, 19 July 1980. It was run off the presses in the dungeonous machine room below Mitchell Street.

The following Monday the Glasgow Herald's first issue to be produced by electronic technology appeared from the paper's new home in Albion Street. Although the potential for disaster in moving a newspaper's production centre overnight from one part of the city to another was enormous, the whole operation went exactly as planned. Newspapermen, with their reputation for scepticism, learned that week-end that miracles can happen.

Without that particular miracle there would probably have been no Glasgow Herald – or Evening Times – today. In the final Mitchell Street years the papers' Victorian machinery was worked out beyond repair. Linotype operators had to set columns of type on machines quite literally held together with bits of string and sticky tape. Too often the papers were printed too late to catch delivery vans or trains simply because the ancient machinery had collapsed under the strain.

This was hardly surprising. Since the days of Caxton the general principle of printing – taking wooden or metal impressions of letters, inking them and stamping them on to paper – had not changed much although periodic advances in automation had speeded up the process.

This simple method had done the Herald proud for most of its two centuries, but by the time that Edition No. 138 in the 198th year of publication came off the presses that night in Mitchell Street everyone in the business knew that the provision of new facilities in another part of Glasgow had not come a moment too soon. There was simply far too

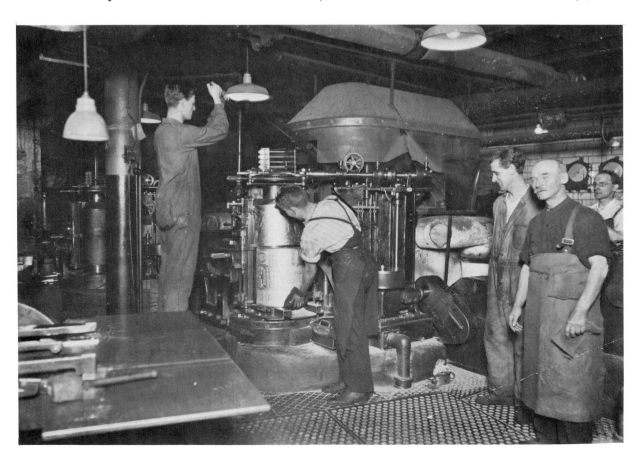

much typesetting to be done on old machinery by a method which was complicated and slow. When machinery broke down there were increasing problems in finding spare parts. This was hardly surprising since some of the machinery in use in 1980 had been installed when the Herald began production in Buchanan Street/Mitchell Street almost 112 years before.

If the effects on the Glasgow Herald were serious, they were even more daunting for the Evening Times, dependent, as are all evening papers, on rapid production and delivery. There is no more pointless occupation than producing newspapers too late for people to buy them.

Not only the machinery was threatening the future of both papers; further obstacles to rapid despatch and delivery of the Glasgow Herald and Evening Times had been provided by the steady encroachment of pedestrian-only streets around the Herald office. Buchanan Street, where in more elegant times the Herald had its imposing entrance, became closed to traffic; Gordon Street was similarly closed and plans were in hand to extend the system to Argyle Street. A time was envisaged when the Herald office would be marooned, cut off from its own delivery fleet. After the Beaverbrook retreat from Glasgow and the subsequent failure of the Scottish Daily News, the Outram management decided to abandon Mitchell Street in favour of the former Scottish Daily Express headquarters in Albion Street.

First the black glass building in Albion Street had to be cleared out completely and restocked with all the complicated spaghetti entrails of electronics. It was an enormous job involving the Outram board in putting £15m into a new future, a significant investment in Glasgow at a time of recession and industrial pessimism. Much of the money went on the ultra-modern computerised technology for typesetting which could do the job quickly, cleanly, silently and in a larger number of type faces.

When the Glasgow Herald left Mitchell Street in that historic flitting the paper said goodbye to several of the printing staff who had been with the company for many years. They were printers of the old school, men with inky elbows and long black overalls who could carry a galley of type like a waiter carries a trayload of champagne glasses, with a surety of movement to make the uninitiated close their eyes in fear; they were men who lived among permanent clattering machinery – comps, upmakers, operators, bulkmen, jobbers and punch operators who lipread each other above the noise. They lived in the world of the flong, mangle, matrix, elrod, chase, stick and slug, and put together their work on a stone (in fact a slab of steel) supported by sturdy legs of old oak.

Now it is all changed. Today the printers arrive for work in their golf gear and sometimes wear white coats which would not look out of place in the funny farm. Their world is one of VDUs, printouts, bromides, inputting and all the other jargon to be found in any other industry using electronics. Nowadays printers are pasters, photo-typesetters and keyboard operators who spend most of their days peering into television screens. Probably the only people who still have ink on their fingers are the men of the machine-room where the paper parcels itself up and presents itself, wrapped and ready, for delivery. The anonymous corridors and open plan uniformity of Albion Street are the price of progress.

Yet there is no denying that the new system is immensely more efficient than before. There are far fewer typographical errors in the papers and deadlines are mostly met safely.

There is nothing new in the search for improvement. When the Glasgow Herald flitted 111 years earlier to Buchanan Street its first edition contained a message from the proprietors which was as apt in 1980 as it was then: 'The circulation of the Herald has extended vastly especially of late years and continues to advance regularly and rapidly.' They too had their production problems. 'So great has been this increase that latterly the Proprietors found it difficult to produce by the Machinery at their command, the number of copies daily demanded by the Public.' Proudly they announced that their new buildings were of a 'singularly commodious kind and adapted in every respect to the requirements of their business', which was exactly the case in 1980.

The same keyboard skills – but
an entirely different process.
Above, casting type in single lines
of metal. Below, the keyboard operator
is directly linked to a large computer.

From its new 'commodious' home in Albion Street the Glasgow Herald welcomed a new era with a front page statement to its readers and explained the reasons for its move from Buchanan Street/Mitchell Street back 'to where it has its roots in the heart of Old Glasgow'. The first issue from Albion Street was noticeably different in shape from that last issue from Mitchell Street. It was broader, with ten columns instead of nine, and slightly shorter, to comply with the measurements of the Albion Street presses. There was more editorial content too.

As the inevitable gremlins were removed from the system and the staff became familiar with the intricacies of the new technology, the paper daily improved in appearance – clearer pictures, better arranged pages: and above all it came out on time to reach the outer areas of circulation in Scotland.

In today's caseroom type is set by computer and the resultant print-out is pasted to a make-up plan and photographed before being screened and placed on a rotary press. This production process, which was brought into operation without enforced redundancies, put the Glasgow Herald ahead of most major newspapers in Britain.

Thus the Glasgow Herald faces its third century better equipped than most and it will need all the technological strengths it can muster to face the challenge of the electronic age. Television, radio and the electronic news services on television all conspire to make fraught the economics of the newspaper industry. There are, however, encouraging signs; in the great economies of the world, notably the United States, Japan and Germany, the technological revolution has not wiped out newspapers as a news and advertising medium despite the prophesies of pessimists. Instead of becoming enslaved by electronics, alert newspapers have made electronics their slave and have survived and prospered.

174

Appendix 4

CHARLES RENNIE MACKINTOSH AND THE GLASGOW HERALD

by John Weyers

The management of George Outram and Company was the first commercial body to give approval to an architectural design in which Charles Rennie Mackintosh played a major part. In return Mackintosh made the Glasgow Herald a landmark in a city already full of outstanding buildings. A pen and ink perspective of the Herald's main frontage, drawn in 1893, is now in the Glasgow University Collection, and it is the earliest example of Mackintosh's professional draughtsmanship to have survived.

Comparisons of the perspective with the completed structure show the minor alterations normal in the construction of a major building, and it is a scholarly debating ground exactly how strict a control the senior partners of Honeyman and Keppie maintained over their young apprentice. Much of the outside of the building has strong and undoubted Mackintosh characteristics – one authority finding that the top floor detail 'has begun to melt and flow under the hot breath of Art Nouveau'.

The corner tower is of especial interest, showing not only the marriage of Business Baronial with the beginnings of the Glasgow Style, but also the influence of Mackintosh's visit to Italy. He had won the coveted Alexander (Greek) Thomson Travelling Scholarship in 1890, within a year of joining Honeyman and Keppie.

The perspective also shows in its sky treatment, unusual for the architecture practice of the day, a hint of the brilliant drawings to follow so much later in life. It is ironic that his short architectural career, which ended in disappointment and failure, should have secured recognition for him as a figure of international stature, yet have overshadowed so many aspects of his later art.

His watercolours alone would have earned him a permanent place in art history, equalling the reputation of his furniture designs. His work with

fabrics, until recently very little known, may earn equal recognition. His genius was still flowering in new fields at an age when his contemporaries in Glasgow were merely repeating the formula with which they found success.

Despite the Herald's first encouragement of Mackintosh, and its approval not only of the building, but acceptance of the furniture he designed, the paper has earned a reputation for attempting to undermine his standing.

It must be accepted that for a considerable period some of the paper's writers mocked the legend. When a demolition gap appeared in Sauchiehall Street, showing the least attractive face of Glasgow's School of Art – a building which is acknowledged to be the crowning achievement of Mackintosh's imagination – it was hoped by one columnist that reconstruction would soon restart to hide it. The Mappin Terraces at London Zoo were called to mind. Even recently one writer regarded it as artistic justice that Mackintosh and his wife Margaret Macdonald had to live with their own furniture and decor.

To a certain extent this was forgivable. Much of Mackintosh's furniture is obviously conceived for visual effect, part of an overall design, rather than with petty considerations of actual use. The Herald staff, unfortunately, never at any period containing a majority of aesthetes, had to use it. Chairs which are uncomfortable, drawers which fall out, and tables which are difficult to sit at, do not breed respect, and an honest criticism of them is not philistinism. The same cannot be said, regrettably, of the then management and a city planning department which allowed the Mitchell Street building to be defaced with signs, or, perhaps, of a newspaper which turned an ineffective eye, if not a blind one, to the destruction of much of the city's architectural heritage.

At an official editorial level, the Herald certainly does not deserve its persisting anti-Mackintosh label. When his memorial exhibition was held in 1933, the Herald's long main report was headed simply 'An Architectural Genius', while in his own assessment the paper's art critic spoke of the extraordinary beauty of some of the exhibits, and the wide range of spheres in which Mackintosh's genius was expressed. Nearly fifty years later, when the Herald was responsible for locating eleven items of 'lost' furniture, one of the owners was so incensed by previous criticism of Mackintosh in the paper that he would speak to the writer of the articles only anonymously, and then dealt through a third party to negotiate terms for the restoration and exhibition of the pieces. In subsequent detective work the Herald located material which has earned display at both the Art School and the Hunterian Art Gallery. It may not have censored anti-Mackintosh views, but on innumerable occasions it has given encouragement to his disciples and evangelists.

Two pieces of oak furniture designed by Mackintosh for the Herald have been presented to Glasgow Art Galleries and Museums by the management of George Outram & Co. The first is a large table, believed to have been designed for editorial conferences, and it is this piece which may have first inspired dislike for his work; it is extremely difficult to find a place for one's feet under the table because of the lower stretchers. The second piece is an interesting confidential filing cabinet, possibly for the Editor's secretary, in which the Glasgow style is very much in evidence.

When the paper moved from Mitchell Street to Albion Street the Editor's room was, of course, left *in situ*. It is hoped at the time of writing to locate this on permanent display, one favourite site being the People's Palace on Glasgow Green. It was in this area that the paper was born; it is here, in the city's Glasgow collection, that the paper's very first handpress is housed.

Appendix 5

WHAT THE HERALD SAID

11 November 1805

DEATH OF LORD NELSON

We have the high satisfaction of communicating to our Readers the intelligence of one of the most important victories that was ever achieved by the gallantry and skill of our seamen. The combined squadrons of France and Spain were engaged by the British Fleet under Lord Nelson on the 21st October and completely defeated, 10 of their ships being left in the hands of the victors. But we have the affliction to add that this victory has been purchased with the life of Lord Nelson. The matchless hero was wounded by a musket ball in the middle of the action and survived but a short time. The loss of such a man at such a time may well be considered a national catastrophe. His memory however will be cherished for ages by his affectionate and grateful nation.

29 June 1815

AFTER WATERLOO

If we were much astonished at the late signal victory over the enemy, considering the means with which it was effected, we are certainly not less so at the great progress made towards Paris by the gallant British and Prussian armies since the ever-memorable battle in question. . . . Without pretending to be acquainted with the precise fact, we can state that it is generally understood the Duke of Wellington on his arrival before Paris, will peremptorily demand, as a sine qua non for peace, Bonaparte to be given up to the Allies and that he would undertake for his safety in England.

19 November 1820

THE TRIAL OF QUEEN CAROLINE IN THE HOUSE OF LORDS

Lord Ellenborough, a member of the Secret Committee, admitted that a great part of the evidence had failed to substantiate the charges against her Majesty. On the whole, however, he conceived that strong suspicions attached to many parts of the Queen's conduct, and that her intimacy with Bergami was deserving of the deepest censure. . . . She has discovered the presumptuous fallacy of those who told her, and we know she was so told, that the domestic enemies of England were strong enough to protect her from justice; that disaffection was so general the Ministers would not dare to pursue the inquiry; and that if they did she might even expect to ascend a *vacant* Throne. These guilty hopes have all vanished and left her a spectacle of deep commiseration.

Her friends, if such we may call them, affect to discover in a majority of only twenty-eight a triumphal acquittal. Miserable sophistry! One hundred and twenty-three British peers pronounce her not only an adultress, but one who has been guilty of gross and licentious conduct, and that solemnly recorded opinion called a virtual acquittal!

20 November 1819

PETERLOO

The meeting at Manchester on Monday last has been attended with disastrous consequences, several lives having been lost and many individuals wounded. . . . In such a state the Magistrates are imperiously called upon to act with energy; for every injury sustained by the peaceable citizen, and the public at large, is laid at their door. Nor even with the most judicious management will they escape animadversion. Should the first appearance of disturbance be quashed by the vigorous conduct of the magistracy there will be an outcry that no danger existed but in the terrified imaginations of our rulers, and that the steps which they took were unnecessarily harsh. Should there, on the other hand, be an unwillingness to interfere, and confusion arise in consequence of this indulgence, then there is a universal censure of the Magistrates; they are accused of want of spirit and foresight, having allowed an evil to get to a height which might have been easily checked at its first appearance, and, in short, of being the authors of all the calamities which ensued.

13 March 1820
CATHOLIC EMANCIPATION
We have formerly said, and we now repeat it, that the concessions to the Catholics, if they are to be given at all, should be given with a good grace and all at once, not leaving room for pretence of future complaint. . . . If we are to have the liegemen of the Pope sitting in our House of Commons, it is quite immaterial whether they be returned by ten-pound or forty-shilling freeholders. The priests, when they choose to interfere, will carry the day with either the one description or the other, and the Pope, through the Bishops, will have equally the nomination wherever his Holiness shall be pleased to exercise it.

2 July 1830
DEATH OF GEORGE IV
He was an amiable man, an accomplished gentleman and a wise king.

11 June 1832
REFORM BILL
After having got everything their own way the Reformers are as dissatisfied as ever. One of their complaints is that the King did not acknowledge their majesty by going in person to give his assent to the Bill, but transmitted it by commission. Another grievance, and they will probably find it a lasting one, is that they are not to be allowed the sole and exclusive nomination of Members of Parliament – Tory demonstrations are presenting themselves in all quarters, especially in the counties; as a proof of which Mr Palmer, the agricultural candidate, has beat Mr Hallett, the Reformer in Berkshire. There is also a very decided split among themselves.

23 June 1837
VICTORIA
At present we feel no inclination to revert to the political events of our departed sovereign's reign; still less are we inclined to speculate upon the political predilections or probable conduct of our youthful Queen. We have observed with more than regret a suspicion insinuated that a dangerous influence is exercised over her. We trust the insinuation is unfounded, but at any rate, now is not the time to dwell upon such a theme. . . . The task which fate has devolved upon her is arduous in the extreme. Let not her difficulties be increased nor her hopes embittered by the display of a premature jealousy when all should be confidence and cordiality.

8 November 1839
OPIUM WAR
The confiscated opium thus sacrificed was delivered by the British owners in obedience to the instructions, and they hold themselves entitled to recompense in the first instance from the British Government. In the meantime, all trade with China continues to be suspended.

28 December 1846
POTATO FAMINE
We only refer to Ireland to say, generally, that the same accounts of wretchedness and famine, riot, robbery, murder, and reckless resolve to live on English charity rather than labour for their own sustenance, or the improvement of their beautiful country, are still furnished, with even additional features of aggravation. Much of this must be attributed to the efforts of O'Connell . . . to keep up the game of Repeal of the Union at all hazards.

17 November 1854
THE CHARGE OF THE LIGHT BRIGADE
The charge of our Light Brigade on the 25th seems to have been made under a misconception of orders. Dearly have our gallant fellows paid for it.

They attacked batteries even at the cannon's mouth. They killed the gunners who manned the Russian guns; but they gained nothing beyond the praise universally bestowed on the brilliancy of their attack. That one man returned alive is esteemed a miracle. The victory however was gained at a price which we are not able at present to state precisely.

27 April 1861
AMERICAN CIVIL WAR

The struggle among the Americans themselves – between the Unionists and the Secessionists – lamentable as it is, has commenced in a much milder form [than Bunker's Hill in the Revolutionary War]; for it appears that though there was a gallant struggle of forty hours' duration before Fort Sumpter fell, the fight has been wondrously innocuous, for we are told that none of the officers of the garrison were wounded, nor were any of the Carolinians killed. Though a great deal of powder and shot was expended, it seems to have done very little harm, and fewer lives were lost than during the Glasgow riots of 1848. This is a very safe sort of warfare, and would be a capital beginning for raw and timid recruits, who would have the chance of smelling powder without the disagreeable accompaniment of seeing blood. It is to be hoped that if the Civil War continues all their battles may be fought as satisfactorily, and without greater danger to life or damage to property.

26 September 1862
INDIAN MUTINY

If the Indian mutiny was the last result of a long series of causes that had been evolving themselves for a hundred years, from the misrule of the East India Company, it will also, it is to be hoped, be the beginning of a new series of causes which shall produce the greatest benefits both to our home interests and to the people of India. No evil is wholly unmixed with good, and the Indian mutiny, which was thought at the time to be the greatest calamity that had befallen our Empire, will undoubtedly be regarded by future Hindu his-

torians as the clearly defined point at which the enlightened intellect of this country was first earnestly brought to bear on the concerns of that part of our Empire.

23 September 1862
SLAVERY

At the present moment the Government of Mr Lincoln is sorely puzzled with a superabundance of 'contraband' and emancipated negroes. They are everywhere present in the land and in the President's calculations; and how they are to be accommodated or got rid of is the perplexing question. They have been seriously advised to take themselves off quietly and found colonies or kingdoms somewhere as soon as they can find time, space and opportunity, providing always that the locality is outside of the United States. Mr Lincoln has plainly intimated to the free coloured people of the North that they are an inferior race, and that white men as a general rule are better pleased with their absence than their company. . . . To many people this policy may appear to be selfish and somewhat unnatural, but Mr Lincoln is not to be blamed for stating the simple truth. It is notorious that Americans have a deep-rooted dislike of the negro population in the North, and no process of reasoning seems capable of transforming that feeling into anything stronger than simple toleration.

6 October 1862
SLAVERY (continued)

President Lincoln proclaims 'that on January 1, 1863, all slaves within any State shall be then, thenceforward and forever free, and the Federal authorities . . . will do no act to repress them in any efforts they may make for their actual freedom.' Here, then, we have the President committed to a policy of slave emancipation. He has hitherto tried to leave the question of slavery or emancipation to be decided by the States themselves. . . . With an extraordinary degree of indecision Mr Lincoln has alternately favoured and discouraged the schemes of the Abolishionists.... In a letter to Horace Greeley, he frankly confessed that the salvation of the Union by any means was his primary consideration and that the question of slavery was to be dealt with as a matter of expediency. If the Union could be saved by upholding slavery then Mr Lincoln was fully prepared to uphold it.

27 April 1865

DEATH OF LINCOLN

All the prominent features of his character, down to his very weaknesses, were amiable; and even his far-famed stories had no grain of ill-nature in them. He was not a genius or a hero and he was probably on that account better fitted to bring the war to a satisfactory conclusion. His loss will be greatly deplored in the North.

14 August 1885

SECRETARY OF STATE FOR SCOTLAND

It seems that, contrary to many expectations, the Duke of Richmond and Gordon, the present President of the Board of Trade, is to be the first Secretary for Scotland. The Bill creating that office has become law, and we are not sure that the Conservatives have made a bad stroke in appointing so distinguished a nobleman and good man of business to fill it.... One thing is almost certain, and that is that the Duke will commit no egregious blunder, nor is he likely to assert to any extreme extent his powers as the Secretary for the northern kingdom. He will do his work modestly and efficiently and with the minimum amount of oratory, the latter always to be considered as a virtue in an administrator.

3 January 1896

THE JAMESON RAID

The Rand may yet have its deliverer. Dr Jameson, however, is not to be the man. He is the Monmouth of the Uitlander revolutionary movement, not its William III. He and his troops were compelled on New Year's Day to surrender to an overwhelming force – whether of military police or of burghers does not quite clearly appear – at Krugersdorp about twenty miles from Johannesburg. There was hard fighting and unfortunately men were killed and wounded on both sides.... Thus rather ignobly ends what there is every reason to believe to have been a purely filibustering expedition.... Messages ordering Jameson to retrace his steps reached him. But he disregarded them and pushed on. This disobedience, of course, deprives him of all sympathy, here or in Cape Colony. Perhaps we shall know ere long what motive of ambition, or maybe of honest but mistaken indignation at Boer barbarity, turned the head of a man whose discretion at the time of the Matabele war appeared as indisputable as his bravery.

22 May 1900

THE POET LAUREATE'S ODE TO MAFEKING

It is sad to see that although our commanders have mended their management of the war, our poets' handling of it is as bad as ever. Had General Baden-Powell conducted the defence of Mafeking no better than Mr Alfred Austin sings it, there would not be so much bunting flying throughout the British Empire today. One can, of course, pardon a good deal when people are in a state of patriotic excitement, and even the police magistrates are rightly lenient to boisterous offenders at a time like this. But Mr Austin really tries our patience a little too far in his ode on the defence of Mafeking, and if the country were as fastidiously artistic as it is fervently patriotic, he might be in some peril from the hands of a critical mob. To tell the truth, it would be difficult to find among the worst verses of the worst Laureates anything more lamentable than this wonderful ode. It is worse even than Mr Austin's own celebration of the Jameson Raid, for while that was only an effort in what may be called the modern colloquial ballad strain, this is a travesty of a noble and famous model. It was, indeed, in an evil hour that the Laureate bethought himself of Drayton's 'Agincourt' and resolved to give us in the measure of it such unspeakably cacophonous lines.

23 January 1901

DEATH OF VICTORIA

When the history of Queen Victoria comes to be written it will probably be found that she was not only the model constitutional Sovereign but the family lawyer of the British Empire. . . . At the time of her death Queen Victoria was the most experienced politician in Europe as well as in Great Britain.

2 June 1902

END OF THE BOER WAR

It has been a long and weary time. . . . It has been marked by as many if not as stupendous vicissitudes as any struggle in which this country has ever been engaged; and it has taxed almost to the last the energies of the largest and best equipped army that this country has been able to send from its shores. . . . Nothing could well be more foolish than to attempt to anticipate the verdict of military history upon the war which has now come to a close. South Africa has been the grave of many military reputations which before 1899 were regarded as unimpeachable. When the censorship and other unprecedented devices for keeping the public uninformed are no longer in evidence we may be certain that the story of the struggle will be rewritten . . . and it is quite clear that 'efficiency' will have to be written not only on but all over the Army Office clean slate in the pressingly immediate future.

7 May 1910

DEATH OF EDWARD VII

Edward VII was probably not the first of British Sovereigns to recognise that the first of British interests is peace. But he was the first to make the doctrine his supreme study and achievement, to bend his energies to its realisation from the outset, and to trust to no hand but his own in securing that it should be universally accepted as the dominating principle of British policy.

5 August 1914

BRITAIN AT WAR

At midnight one of the most critical hours in Britain's history struck. . . . We shall not try to anticipate the verdict which history will pronounce on the diplomatic mysteries which have had this terrible issue. But if judgement is in suspense on the question of responsibility for this war of the nations, our grounds for suspecting that Germany deliberately rendered a rupture of the peace of Europe inevitable are not irrational. . . . History may ultimately declare that the gods first made mad those whom they meant to destroy. But if the facts are as we have read them it would seem that Germany has pursued Bismark's policy of provoking a war and then taunting the enemy with the charge of wanton aggression.

8 January 1916

CONSCRIPTION

(Sir John Simon having referred to the measure just introduced in Parliament as 'an imitation of Prussian militarism'.)

The important point is that the Militia Acts are the legal recognition of a principle traceable through the whole of English and Scottish history that it is the duty of every man of military age to defend his country. The only important circumstance which differentiates the present Bill from any preceding enactments is the fact that the defence of this country is being made on foreign soil, and the unanswerable reply to that argument is that if it is not made abroad it will ultimately have to be made at home. The proposal now before Parliament is certainly no 'imitation of Prussian militarism' but a continuous national tradition.

2 May 1916

THE EASTER RISING

After a week of anarchy, the Dublin rebels have capitulated. . . . It will take some little time, no doubt, to stamp out the insurrectionary fires throughout the distressful country, but the movement of the establishment of an Irish Republic under the auspices of Kaiser Wilhelm is as dead as Napper Tandy.... Let it be remembered that Germany's sins of commission enter conspicuously into this tragic episode. It is observable that the German press has treated the outbreak in a very sketchy fashion. Nothing has been allowed to appear in print that would connect Germany with the game of gun-running, and the adventurous voyage of Sir Roger Casement.... Unfortunately for the success of this blandly impudent attempt to deceive, neutral countries are not all ill-informed, nor are they ignorant of the designs which Germany cherished in reference to an island which ... was indispensable to Germany's command of the seas.

12 November 1918
IT IS FINISHED
If in the course of these years of conflict human nature has never been seen to sink so low, never, following the subtle laws of compensation has it risen to such sublime heights.... Our reading of this war is the triumph of a mighty moral crusade and the vindication of religion as the most vital influence on the world stage.... Germany and Germany's allies have been abased. In the record of mankind their humiliation will go for little. What counts is that the cause for which these our enemies stood, the systems they represented, the doctrines they defended, the whole perverted attitude towards humanity and human rights and liberties which they maintained have gone, and, as we believe, for ever.

23 January 1924
THE FIRST LABOUR GOVERNMENT
Prominent in the new Cabinet are three members of the Upper House – Lord Parmoor, Lord Haldane (who returns to the Woolsack), and Viscount Chelmsford, a Unionist who has been Viceroy of India and will enjoy the distinction of being the First Lord of the Admiralty in the first Socialist Administration the country has known. Mr Ramsay Macdonald has thus refrained from gratifying the membership of the House of Lords by the elevation of some of the *pur sang* of Labour and Socialism to the honourable role of Elder Statesmen. We shall never be able to suspect this branch of the Administration of affinities with Lenin and Trotsky so long as it remains the most remarkable example our politics has yet produced of orthodoxy and heterodoxy mixed – as the painter said of his masterpiece – with brains. For Lord Chelmsford, as has been mentioned, is a Conservative, while Lord Parmoor, the new Lord President of the Council, is not only a Conservative, but, *mirabile dictu,* a member of the Carlton Club. Truly we live in strange times when the very fount and source of Diehardism can be convicted of producing such a phenomenon as a Socialist Lord President! As for Lord Haldane who, the other day, was one of the most distinguished Liberal statesmen, it seems to us that he confers more lustre upon the Socialist Party than it confers upon him. Unquestionably however the presence of these men in the new Cabinet carries with it a measure of reassurance.

3 May 1926
GENERAL STRIKE
The country is faced today with the threat of a general strike beginning at midnight.... To yield would be to end the days of constitutional government in Britain. Even if the strikers returned to work after a settlement of the coal dispute had been secured in accordance with the miners' demands, only the appearance of normal condition would be restored. The General Council of the Trades Union Congress would have successfully asserted its prior lien on the loyalty of trade unionists and the precedent of invoking its authority and command of brute force would have been established. Inevitably the general strike weapon would be employed again, probably on some occasion of less moment, and the process would be repeated until the bolder of the leaders at length decided on the coup d'état which it is apparent from Mr Wheatley's speech in Glasgow yesterday is already present in the thoughts of the extremists, and set out to possess themselves of the symbols as well as the realities of power. Then would dawn for Britain the day of the dictatorship of the proletariat.

20 May 1926
AFTER THE GENERAL STRIKE

Mr Ramsay Macdonald is on fairly safe ground in predicting that a general strike will not be heard again in the lifetime of people now of mature age. One may go further, indeed, and express a hope that the national experiences of the past few weeks will have condensed themselves into a universally accepted principle, namely that the general strike belongs to the same category of obsolete crudities as the methods of the old sectarians who 'proved their doctrine orthodox by apostolic blows and knocks'. A general strike can have no raison d'être save as a prelude to revolution. As an industrial weapon it is a boomerang which returns at once and with deadly force upon the poorest of those classes on whose behalf it was ostensibly wielded.

23 May 1927
LINDBERGH

To have accomplished a flight from New York to Paris, alone in a monoplane, is one of the brilliant feats of aviation, and an adventure that will stir the blood of the most unromantically minded . . . with so much healthy rivalry between the nations in aerial progress Captain Lindbergh has scored heavily for the United States. No one will grudge him his triumph. . . . Some will be found to ask what useful purpose has been served by this flight. At present the airoplane is poorly fitted for crossing the Atlantic. The probability is that when aerial communication is established between Europe and America the airship will come into its own. The airship possesses marked advantages for long distance flying: it carries more engines than the airplane, has more space for fuel, and is better fitted for fighting bad weather. Yet the airoplane's progress may make it in future years a much stronger rival to the airship for long distance flight. . . . But in the end this single-handed flight will be remembered as another successful endeavour to do what no man has done before and to assert the supremacy of man over nature.

31 January 1933
HITLER AS CHANCELLOR

. . . . It is said that the revolutionary Adolf Hitler has undertaken to govern constitutionally. . . . What is perhaps more to the point is that . . . Herr Hitler can command in addition to the Reichswehr, the Nazi 'storm troops' and the 250,000 members of the Stahlhelm who adhere to the nationalist cause. There can be no question that Germany has taken a large step towards a new form of government. . . . If the constitution obstructs [his] purposes it can only be a matter of time before it is remodelled, regularly or irregularly. . . . The Nazi leader has still to prove himself a statesman; as a politician he must be admitted to have few equals.

11 December 1936
ABDICATION

. . . . Even a few weeks ago the suggestion that a reign begun under the happiest of auspices might abruptly terminate in the midst of a national crisis would have been received with frank incredulity. But the events of the past week had prepared the nation for yesterday's announcement; and although there is deep disappointment and profound regret at the decision King Edward has felt impelled to take, the universal tendency is to accept the inevitable without controversy and quietly to prepare for a stable future under the new regime. There was a period in the beginning of the present week when there appeared to be a danger of the situation leading to acute divisions of opinion in the country. But the correctness of King Edward's attitude and the statesmanship displayed by the Prime Minister stemmed the flood of rumour and innuendo and enabled the nation to face developments calmly and with a proper appreciation of the issues involved. . . . When the project of a morganatic marriage was rejected His Majesty realised at once that the choice before him was limited to the two simple alternatives – abandonment of the association and continuance on the throne, or abdication and freedom to make Mrs Simpson his wife.

In a world where there are nearly as many opinions as there are individuals, King Edward's preference for the latter course will not escape criticism. But from those who have given him their affectionate loyalty he is surely entitled to expect sympathy and understanding.

7 September 1935

FIVE MILES A MINUTE

Sir Malcolm Campbell continues to excel himself. Not content with the speed of 276.816 miles per hour set up at Daytona in March, his restless spirit set to work again to have his Bluebird prepared for another attempt, and yesterday on the salt flats of Utah he at last exceeded 300 miles an hour. A man – albeit an exceptional individual – has travelled over the ground at the rate of five miles a minute. It is an astounding thought, especially since the air speed record for land planes stands at almost the same figure. Perhaps the ordinary motorist may best realise the performance if he thinks of it as ten times the speed at which, if he is an honest man, he passes through the restricted areas. No matter how the ordeal is considered, it is amazing to contemplate. We notice that Lord Wakefield in his cable of congratulations appeals to Sir Malcolm Campbell to rest on his laurels. Most of us will echo the sentiment, but not with overmuch faith that it will be heard. On the last occasion on which Sir Malcolm Campbell thought it necessary to break his own record Lord Wakefield said much the same thing. . . . Our generation may have its fill of speed before it is done. So he would be sanguine who believed that the salt flats will lose their savour after this performance. If Sir Malcolm Campbell does not tempt them again someone else will.

Sir Malcolm Campbell on land and water in his famous Bluebirds.

4 September 1939

STANDING FIRM

.... Today we have counted the cost. The thought of war brings nothing of the false exhilaration which is too apt to spring from a half acknowledged assumption that the suffering of war will fall on a minority, and that the cheering majority will reap only a vicarious glory. For some of us, indeed, there may be a certain sense of relief — relief that the long tension of waiting is over and that Britain has chosen in the way of honour and future security.... We may count ourselves fortunate that today there is no German Fleet strong enough to threaten seriously the British command of our home waters or to challenge the position of British squadrons on the wider seas of the world, as Admiral von Speer's ships were able to do in the Pacific twenty-five years ago.

5 June 1940

OUT OF THE NET

As they read or listened to Mr Churchill's account of the great evacuation from Dunkirk, the memories of many Scots must have caught an echo of the most stirring of our metrical psalms:

> Even as a bird
> Out of the fowler's snare
> Escapes away,
> So is our soul set free.
> Broke are their nets
> And thus escaped we.

The same day

CABINET COORDINATION

For many months before Mr Churchill took over the Premiership from Mr Chamberlain, there was a vocal and growing demand for a reorganisation of the War Cabinet. It was pointed out that the members of the Cabinet were both too many and too heavily burdened with purely departmental duties. Our recent experience has dolefully confirmed the weight of these arguments. It is now only too clear that during the months of 'Sitzkrieg' which the Nazi enemy used to perfect and enlarge his formidable war machine, many things were left undone on our side which ought to have been done and which could have been done given vigour of the sort that Mr Churchill and his new colleagues are bringing to our preparations.... The first necessity is that the red-tapism and easy going methods of the recent past should be finally abandoned.

13 March 1941

LEASE LEND

In some ways the passing of the Lease and Lend Act and President Roosevelt's instant action to bring it into full force are the most encouraging things that have happened since this war began. They are as important to our cause as the crushing defeat of the German daylight air attacks last year, General Wavell's victories in Africa, or the heroic stand of Greece. It is true that without these successes we might never have won this American support. It had to be earned, for though President Roosevelt is one of the most convinced and consistent foes of totalitarian tyranny, and though the sympathy of United States citizens was behind in growing strength from the moment when the war ceased to seem 'phoney' in American eyes, we could not have hoped for much solid help so long as there was any doubt about our capacity to fight for ourselves not only bravely but successfully. In a world as full of dangers as ours is no country dare back a loser and so invite the revenge of brutal aggressors. It is because the American people believe that, given a reasonable chance, we can win that the United States is now going to supply us on a scale never equalled in past wars. But this truth does not reduce in any way the significance of our friends' action, or the gratitude that we are bound to feel for it.

16 February 1942

SINGAPORE FALLS

The British people are not so inured to the shock of disaster that they will regard the loss of Singapore as one of the inevitable misfortunes of war.

. . . This is no time to list the chronicle of disaster or to apportion the blame. It is, however, legitimate to ask questions to which answers must be given or a character that will ensure that similar questions will not again become pertinent. For example, nine days before Singapore capitulated General Percival stated categorically that the forces under his command would hold it. If that claim was a gesture of defiance to the enemy, or an attempt to stiffen civilian morale there and elsewhere, it might carry some justification, although it should not have been so unequivocally phrased. But if General Percival's confidence was based on a wrong appreciation of the military situation it is wholly inexcusable. Again it may with justice be asked why the causeway between the mainland and the island was not destroyed. No doubt the causeway was less susceptible to scorched earth treatment than, say, an oil well. But it should have been obvious two months ago that Singapore was Japan's objective. Therefore the elementary precautions should have been taken of mining almost the entire length of the causeway, so that it could be breached in a dozen places. Can it be that too much reliance was placed on our defending batteries, although these batteries were assuredly scheduled as targets for Japanese bombers? Once again it would seem that there has been a failure in direction in the coordination of military and civilian effort.

7 June 1944
SECOND FRONT
The long awaited attack has begun. . . . At sea the strength of the German Navy has been so seriously diminished that the enemy can hardly be expected to be much more than a nuisance. . . . The Second Front is three dimensional war, but it seems probable that the decisive blows will be struck on land. This terrain is certain to be strongly contested. . . . The Germans have used it as a training ground for four years, they have taken over and improved the French airfields and other defences, and the possession of Paris means more to them politically and militarily than Rome. Their difficulty is presumably that they could not be certain at first whether the Allied landing at Caen was a feint. . . . We now look forward to the issue with seriousness indeed, but with confident hope for the success of our arms and the just cause for which we are fighting.

11 May 1945
VICTORY AND PEACE
The formal signature by General Keitel in Berlin of Germany's unconditional surrender to the Allies formed a perfect dramatic contrast to the opening of the campaign which was to smash Russia beyond recovery four years ago. . . . It would not be very surprising if our good Russian allies were to lose their heads a little for their triumph has been as spectacular as their peril was great. . . . That victory has been won by all the Allies in concert and it is idle to discuss which has played the greater part. Each has done his utmost and there is glory enough for all. Until patient history sifts out the detail we may let that suffice: for the moment, more urgent tasks await us, and the comradeship in arms must remain cooperation in peace. Germany has to be controlled, rebuilt, and her people re-educated to a sense of human values which they have lost.

27 July 1945
LABOUR'S VICTORY
The first reaction of the country to the verdict of the polls, apart from a sense of stupefied surprise at the wholesome change in the political composition of the new parliament, will be one of profound regret that it should coincide with the Potsdam Conference and the legacy of chaos left by the war. Apart from the unique prestige of Mr Churchill as War Minister and the architect of victory, which has raised him to a position hardly equalled by Chatham and the younger Pitt, the Government which was defeated yesterday had many men of talent and long experience whose word carried weight in every foreign country. With the best will in the world their successors in the Labour Party cannot claim that experience of affairs either at

home or abroad, and unless and until they prove themselves the equals of Mr Churchill and Mr Eden, they will wield less authority in international councils than their predecessors.

8 August 1945
ATOMIC BOMBS AND WORLD ORDER
The atomic bomb is the first practical result of the researches into the structure of the atom begun by Thomson at Cambridge nearly half a century ago. . . . The fact that the end happens to be destructive is accidental though certainly not irrelevant. Science is concerned with discovery, not the ends to which discovery is put; arsenic has saved more lives in the hands of the physician than it has destroyed in the hands of the assassin. . . . It is no use politicians talking of national claims while the peoples face international chaos; a new world order is overdue and it may be that the atomic bomb will compel its formation and its energy constructively used should facilitate progress. But if we do not revolutionise our attitude and control our passions they will control and in the end destroy us.

6 March 1953
DEATH OF A TYRANT
. . . . It might seem impossible that death [of Stalin] has suddenly made men free, as if at once a terrible weight had been removed and a terrible gap created. . . . It is as though for an instant the world stands still in the knowledge that when it moves again everything will be different. . . . In the lands of the West, the objects at once of his hate and of his ambition, there can be no real regret at his passing; if we have lost the faith that made intelligible the phrase 'the scourge of God' we have no reason to doubt either the power or the terror of the scourge which he wielded with a cynical despite of humanity such as Attila might admire. . . . And yet there must be a strange sense of deprivation; that sense that cannot but overtake thoughtful men confronted by the twin facts that the evil that they know is gone and that the evil they do not know remains to be faced.

2 June 1953
THE CONQUEST OF EVEREST
Everest has been conquered. There could be no more dramatic and appropriate news on the eve of the Coronation. . . . It is fitting that of the pair who reached the summit one was a Sherpa, Tensing who was already one of two men who had reached the highest point previously attained. It was no less fitting, and especially appropriate in this Coronation week, that the other climber was E.P. Hillary of New Zealand. This is a tale of great endeavour and resolution . . . true no matter what aid science has provided . . . science can offer only a limited assistance to the man on the mountain. In the final reckoning the highest praise must go to the men who stood on the highest point yet reached by man on foot. . . . The whole world will applaud that the new Elizabethan Age has opened with a demonstration that the qualities displayed by Drake and Raleigh are triumphantly present in the Britain of today.

7 December 1956
WHAT ALTERNATIVE?
The verdict of history on the Suez incident may well be that this was something Britain and France had to do, be the consequences what they might be. . . . Critics of the Government should be quite realistic. There was no alternative to immediate Anglo-French intervention. . . . That the Suez incident provided Russia with a convenient smokescreen for its orgies in Hungary is true and regrettable. It is not a conclusive reason however why Britain and France should not have acted effectively to stop an Israeli-Egyptian war which, but for their action, would have become a general Arab-Israeli war with, we may assume, Russian volunteers intervening.

7 October 1957
OMEN IN ORBIT
Two years ago, President Eisenhower announced America's artificial satellite programme for the International Geo-Physical Year. Almost immedi-

ately the Russians came forward with their own plans; and the race for space was on. Now the Russians have won hands down and ahead of schedule. The first satellite has entered space, a lusty 180 pounder orbiting the earth at 17,000 m.p.h. and peep-peeping impartially on Moscow and Manchester. The event is a landmark in man's technical progress, and it would be churlish to withhold from Soviet scientists the congratulations they undoubtedly deserve. It is, of course, disquieting that the Russians are so much ahead of the West in rocket engineering. The art of putting satellites in orbit has unpleasant affinities with that of launching inter-continental missiles.

23 November 1963
JOHN F. KENNEDY
The death of John F. Kennedy is not just an American but an international disaster. He was only in the third year of a first Presidential term, and he had already made his mark on history, and earned the gratitude and the respect of the whole Western alliance. It was not only the West which had learned to respect him. He had faced, during the tense days and nights of the Cuban crisis, such a strain as few men will ever experience. He had, by his nerve and judgement then, led the world over the watershed of the Cold War. He was the Captain Courageous of the Western alliance, the true friend of Britain, and the embodiment of all that is greatest in the tradition of the American Presidency.

25 January 1965
CHURCHILL
There was something rock-like, so enduring, about the personality of Sir Winston Churchill that the news of his death, even in the fullness of years, is hard to comprehend. He came to represent for the whole Western world the promontory against which the totalitarian tides of the twentieth century surged and broke in vain. . . . Churchill's uniqueness lay in the versatility of his genius: eloquence as well as acumen: historian as well as parliamentarian: artist as well as soldier: nationalist and internationalist combined. . . . None of the lessons of a wide and often hazardous experience of life escaped him. But it was the good fortune of his country that he should have arrived at a well-seasoned political maturity at precisely the moment when his particular combination of courage, wisdom, and humanity was most needed and most rare in the Chancellories of the world.

12 November 1965
NOT ENEMIES
This is a situation for sorrow not for anger. The quarrel between London and Salisbury has reached its logical conclusion. The Rhodesians have stepped into the unknown as bold or as reckless as the first pioneer columns. . . . But now that the British Government's deterrents have failed the task for the country is to limit as far as possible the evil which the Rhodesian decision may breed and to keep open the lines of communication and hopes of reconciliation. . . . The Rhodesians are, de facto, rulers of their own country – indeed, if Britain were dealing with a foreign Power not a technical case of 'rebellion' the Rhodesian government would probably have to wait only a few days for formal recognition. . . . There should be no attempt to cut off all trade with Rhodesia; there should be no threats however faint of British military force. Finally, nothing should be done by the British Government to prevent free movement in and out of Rhodesia. A break-down of relations and a declaration of independence, illegal though it is, does not turn friends into enemies.

Index

Page numbers in *italic* figures
refer to illustration captions.

Street dress, 50 years apart: two pictures that sum it all up.